In fond memory of

Martha L. Stoltz

my teacher, my mentor and friend

Red Squirrel

White Daisy

Blue Heron

Kansas Flora and Fauna in Verse

Steven B. Moon

Contents

Species (Continued)

Jayhawk	*Jayhawkornis kansasensis*
Jayhawk=2	
Killdeer	*Charadrius vociferus*
Little Bluestem	*Andropogon scoparius*
Meadowlark	*Sturnella neglecta*
Mead's Milkweed	*Asclepias meadii*
Monarch Butterfly	*Danaus plexippus*
Muskrat	*Ondatra zibethicus*
Northern Bobwhite	*Colinus virginianus*
Northern Water Snake	*Nerodia sipedon*
Opossum	*Didelphis virginiana*
Ornate Box Turtle	*Terrapene ornata*
Osage-Orange	*Maclura pomifera*
Oxeye Daisy	*Crysanthemum leucanthemum*
Penstemon	*Penstemon buckleyi*
Prairie Coneflower	*Retibida columnifera*
Prairie Phlox	*Phlox pilosa*
Purple Coneflower	*Echinacea purpurea*
Raccoon	*Procyon lotor*
Red Fox	*Vulpes vulpes*
Red Oak	*Quercus rubra*
Red-Tailed Hawk	*Buteo jamaicensis*
Red-Winged Blackbird	*Agelaius phoeniceus*
Ring-Necked Pheasant	*Phasianus colchicus*
Sandhill Crane	*Grus canadensis*
Sand-Hill Plum	*Prunus angustifolia*
Shagbark Hickory	*Carya ovata*
Skunk	*Mephitus mephitus*
Smallflower Verbena	*Verbena bipinnatifida*
Snapping Turtle	*Chelydra serpentina*
Sunflower	*Helianthus annuus*
Sycamore	*Platanus occidentalis*
Timber Rattlesnake	*Crotalus horridus*
Turkey Vulture	*Cathartes aura*
Upland Sandpiper	*Bartramia longicauda*
Virginia Creeper	*Parthenocissus quinquefolia*
Wavyleaf Thistle	*Cirsium undulatum*
Western Painted Turtle	*Chrysemys picta belli*
White-Tailed Deer	*Odocoileus virginianus*

Glossary
Appendices
Author Biography

Acknowledgments

I'd like to thank my wife, Sandy, for all her support and encouragement while I was writing this collection. She has helped me through many times of adversity, as well as my various obsessions du jour. As an English teacher, she also helped with wording and grammar.

I'd also like to thank my daughter and son in law, Kylee and Scott Sharp for their assistance in establishing the list of species to be profiled, plus other technical advice. My younger daughter, Ashley, also provided support and encouragement throughout the writing process.

Several of my fraternity pledge brothers were also helpful in their often blunt criticism. Through their good natured input, they kept me grounded and with their encouragement, kept me working. Of particular mention was Howard Forsythe who was persistent in prodding me to complete and publish the work.

Foreward

I've been asked why I decided to write this style of poetry. I don't have a good answer. I suppose to understand, you'd have to know a bit about me. My immediate family took it in stride - they know me pretty well. My fraternity brothers, however, were much more direct and much less diplomatic, but even they and a few other confidants quickly endorsed the project. I greatly appreciate all the support I received from everyone who was privy to this "off the wall" endeavor.

From early childhood, I've been interested in the outdoors and all things scientific. In high school, I took all the chemistry, physics, math and English that I could. Through a degree in education, with a concentration in science, and subsequently a degree in pharmacy, I took courses in a wide variety of scientific disciplines but never lost my love of nature and biology.

I've always enjoyed reading, everything from the classics to modern novels. I like a good story, but I revel in a story that is laced with learning opportunities. My favorite authors are Arthur C. Clarke, James A. Michener, Patrick O'Brien and Tom Clancy. I also enjoy poetry, but it must at least rhyme, have a definite meter and say something that touches me.

Having lived all my life in Kansas, I especially like the late summer, when the sunflowers are at the height of their beauty. My favorite scene is of bright yellow sunflowers against the clear, blue Kansas sky.

On the way to work one late August morning in 2006, I decided to try to write a poem about a sunflower. I felt that there were already "poems lovely as a tree," and about a ". . . blithe Spirit! Bird thou never wert," so I decided to follow in the footsteps of my favorite authors and include as much factual information as possible. The Sunflower was the first in this series. That poem led me to include other species of Kansas flora and fauna. Almost two years later, I reached the end of the project.

I don't claim to be an expert in the natural history of Kansas. With the help of my biology teacher daughter, we developed a list of significant species and I researched them using multiple sources. I then combined that information with what I learned in all those science classes in college. The seventy seven poems that follow are the fruits of my effort. I hope you enjoy reading them as much as I enjoyed writing them.

S. B. M.

The American Bison

The *Bison bison,* redundant in name,
Is the largest land mammal of American game.
It's commonly known as our own buffalo,
But diverged from that group a long time ago.

They came to this land across Bering Strait.
No one could recall such a magnificent pate.
Curved horns for protection and fighting for status,
Another newcomer, not persona non gratas.

Subspecies exist with large heads and small rumps;
You tell them apart by the size of their humps.
The wood bison's larger and lives amid the trees,
While the smaller plains bison lives out in the breeze.

At two meters tall and three meters long
They go where they want; who'll say they are wrong?
The largest of specimens weighs near a ton.
They're kings of the prairies, for rivals, there's none.

The bison, a keystone upon the Great Plains;
But how'd they achieve it? The question remains.
It's thought that the natives kept numbers in tow;
With decline of plains Indians, the great herds did grow.

Professional hunters, like Buffalo Bill,
Turned the ground red, so great was their skill.
So many were killed, it was a great pity,
But one bison hide brought three bucks in Dodge City.

Seventy million once numbered the herd,
But by 1900, just ten to the third.
Federal protection and herd restoration
Provided recovery; a gift to the nation.

The American Crow

Corvus brachyrhynchos, the American Crow,
Has become the epitome of trouble and woe.
Their feathers are black, with blue iridescence;
They seem to glow with an eerie fluorescence.

From arctic to gulf and ocean to ocean,
They chatter and comment and make a commotion.
In farmland and woodland, in cities and towns,
There's hardly a place where you won't hear their sounds.

They're very omnivorous when it comes to their diet;
If they've never before seen it, they're ready to try it.
They'll eat nestlings and worms, carrion and scraps,
Corn, fish and discarded french fries, perhaps.

They build large stick nests, mostly in trees,
But will also use bushes, whenever they please.
Siblings will stay near their ancestral home
To help raise new fledglings and seldom will roam.

They have many nuances in their vocal display,
From defense and alert to just chattering away.
They also have specialized calls to the troops,
Whenever a predator endangers the group.

They are known to have softer and variable coos
That only within the close family are used.
Primarily they're used for bonding and greeting
And whenever the family members are meeting.

The crow is quite vocal and can mimic the sounds
Of birds and of humans, it just knows no bounds.
The crow's not a raven and won't be a bore,
So you'll never hear this bird cry out, "Nevermore."

The American Hackberry

Celtis occidentalis is the American Hackberry.
It's found nationwide, including the prairie.
As a member in good standing of the family of elm,
There are five different species in the hackberry realm.

It'll reach seventy feet tall and fifty feet wide,
With some of the best shade a tree can provide.
It has ridges and warts of cork in the bark;
It's so very unique, you'll have to remark.

It much prefers soil that's both moist and rich,
But will grow anywhere it secures a small niche.
Vary the moisture, pH or compaction;
A hackberry will grow to your satisfaction.

The serrated, ovate leaves are four inches long,
Much like the elms, to which it belongs.
The twigs show a modestly zig-zag array.
They're light brown when young, but when older, turn gray.

The berries are fleshy and turn purple in fall.
They're consumed by our feathered friends, both large and small.
The seeds are disbursed while the birds move about
And where the seed lands, comes a hackberry sprout.

There isn't much use for hackberry wood,
It's soft and it rots; it's commercially no good.
It produces fine shade, but one thing I'll concede:
It may be a tree, but it's mostly a weed.

The Beaver
(Appendix A)

Castor canadensis is the industrious Beaver.
In the animal world, it's an over achiever.
It likes to build dams in the valleys of streams
To form wetlands and marshes in which other life teems.

They pair up for life; it's not just a fling,
And have up to four kits the following spring.
The kits will stay on for a couple of years
And help with the rearing of new, younger peers.

Relocating beavers is often for naught
'Cause neighboring beavers will move into the spot.
Some people say, "let's just bump off the critters."
But the beavers respond by having large litters.

They learn much by instinct and by imitation.
They learn from their parents a beaver vocation.
They'll learn to build dams, which give them protection,
As well as a larder for their food collection.

The dams will be built with sticks, rocks and mud,
Several feet in height so the valley will flood.
The lodge will have several places to enter
With a den near the top so they'll stay warm through the winter.

Based on the current, they'll vary the dam,
As though they had passed an engineering exam.
It's built straight across when the water is slow,
But curved to withstand the force of more flow.

Both flora and fauna depend on the pond
To provide for their needs, both now and beyond.
Trees, reeds and cattails will border the site,
While fish, birds and waterfowl dwell with delight.

They also exist where dams aren't required,
Because man has provided the pool that's desired.
Dams built by man to service his needs
Provide water for beavers to frolic and breed.

One favorite time that I'll always remember
Is canoeing Neosho, late in November.
With air crisp and cold and the moon full and bright,
Broad tails spanked the water as beavers took flight.

11

Big Bluestem

Andropogon gerardii grows throughout the Great Plains.
It's known as Big Bluestem, but has variant strains.
The stem, at maturity, turns deep purple blue
And the plant grows so tall it inhibits your view.

Big Bluestem's the tallest of grass in its class.
So preferred by the bison, it's called "ice cream grass."
It's considered good forage for all livestock grazing,
And for "natural looks," landscapers are praising.

Three spike-like projections configure the head,
Thus it's called "turkey foot", or so I have read.
It grows in a bunch; sends out rhizomes to spread,
The sod is so strong, to plow it you'll dread.

It attains a majestic three meters in height;
You'll not see too far in it, try as you might.
You can stand on your tip-toes, or try jumping, of course;
If you want to see very far, stand on your horse.

The Big Brown Bat

Eptesicus fuscus is the Kansas Brown Bat.
It's loved just as much as the snake and black cat.
Eptesicus is Greek, translated "house flyers."
With access to buildings, it moves in and retires.

With thirty two teeth, it inflicts a fierce bite,
But catches bugs skillfully, while still in mid-flight.
It's chocolate to red with black face and ears
To see one up close can surely raise fears.

You'll find them in cities and wide open spaces,
But they generally refuse to use forests for bases.
They live in dark sewers, mines, hollow trees,
Or in houses or silos, wherever they please.

They mate in the fall, before hibernation.
The female gives birth after two months gestation.
Conception's delayed until early spring
So young can mature and quickly take wing.

The big brown bat can live to nineteen,
But most die the first winter, or so it would seem.
If not fat enough before winter's sleep,
They'll die in their roost and fall in a heap.

Volleys of calls through their mouths are emitted
To create an "image" from sound so transmitted.
This "echolocation" is used to catch prey
And avoid all the objects that get in the way.

The bat's insectivorous and uses sharp teeth
To crunch through a beetle's chitinous sheath.
They'll eat other bugs, like wasps, moths and flies
But a big, crunchy beetle is still the first prize.

We know vampires are bats, when starting to prey,
And think we'll eat garlic to keep them away.
When confronted by bats, folks still run for cover
As though Bela Lugosi were starting to hover.

The Black Rat Snake
(Appendix B)

Pantherophis obsoleta obsoleta is Black Rat Snake
That it's a beautiful creature, there is no mistake.
The Black Rat can grow over six feet long
With a body that's slender, powerful and strong.

Small rodents are the Rat Snakes primary fare,
But taking young birds is surely not rare.
They kill by constriction, they wrap 'round their prey,
And squeeze out the air till its life slips away.

They're surprisingly skillful at climbing the trees,
Looking for birds and prey they can seize.
They'll climb up in barns for succulent mice
Or will stay on the ground, if that will suffice.

When mating, the male will line up with his bride
And wrap their two tails so their vents will collide.
Into her cloaca he'll insert his hemipenes
In minutes to hours, he'll transfer his genes.

Fifteen plus eggs are laid in five weeks
In a spot where a predator hopefully won't peek.
The young will hatch out in seventy days
To begin their long journey through life's trying maze.

The hatchlings are gray with blotches on their backs,
But when they're adults, they're totally black.
The young can be mistaken for fierce copperheads,
But, rather than copper, they're gray/black instead.

They avoid confrontation and tend to be shy,
However, on this action, you'd best not rely.
They'll vibrate their tails in dry leaves, rattle-like;
With more provocation, you'll find that they strike.

Due to its size, this friend's often killed
By those who think serpents are best when they're stilled.
Without the Black Rat Snake, we'd pay a high price
For keeping in check all the big rats and mice.

The Black Walnut

Juglans nigra is the big walnut, black;
A coveted tree, for uses there's no lack.
In Kansas, you won't find it much in the west,
But profuse in the east where the walnut grows best.

Deep, moist and fertile soil is what it calls home.
It grows best on sandy or silt textured loam.
It's drawn to these soils because they hold water
That it can draw on when strong winds blow hotter.

It much prefers neighbors, a diverse group of folk,
Like hackberry, elm and hickory and oak.
It produces a toxin, a substance called juglone
That keeps away other trees, especially with cones.

The seeds are called nuts, in spite of the covers
The fruit is a drupe, just like many others.
A drupe is a seed with fleshy outsides
Like peaches and cherries and pecans with tough hides.

The tree grows quite tall, near one hundred feet.
The crown is as wide, but the tree is not neat.
The large leaves are alternate, pinnately compound
And produce lots of litter when they fall to the ground.

The walnut's so prized for its valuable lumber,
"Tree rustlers" will strike with owners at slumber.
To walnut tree owners: don't live in a cocoon
Or the trees will become logs by the dark of the moon.

The Black Willow

Salix nigra is the Black Willow tree
That likes its soil to be soaking.
You'll find it near streams where water runs free
Or near ponds where the bull frogs are croaking.

It's a dioecious plant, each tree has one gender,
And it's pollinated by honey bees.
Flowers, which are borne on catkins so slender,
Yield cottony seeds to the breeze.

Its leaves have a simple and lanceolate mien,
With a finely serrated margin.
On top, they are shiny and fairly dark green;
Below, there's a lighter green skin.

It will grow up to fifteen meters in height
With a spreading, irregular head.
It finds the brisk Kansas breeze a delight;
Not breaking, but bending instead.

The tree can be used for those arrows and slings
Which man has been known to fall heir to.
Infections and pains, inflammation and things
Have been treated with Black Willow brew.

Branches can be woven into basket or bowl
And furniture made from the shoots.
But the willow's main use is erosion control,
With stream banks held fast by its roots.

The Black-Tailed Jack Rabbit

Lepus californicus melanotis is the Black-Tailed Jack Rabbit,
Though hare is its more accurate class.
They're found throughout Kansas, but mostly inhabit
The West Kansas plains of short grass.

Their long feet and ears make them a hare,
As well as their precocial kits.
These bunnies are born with a full pelt of hair.
In a month, they survive by their wits.

His big ears are nigh as long as his foot,
With patches of black hair at the ends.
They look like two feathers that he might have put
In his hair like his Plains Indian friends.

Blood's close to the skin in each over-sized ear,
A trait that you'll find very neat.
You know, of course, that they help him to hear,
And they help keep him cool in the heat.

They're mostly nocturnal when they forage for fare,
But they're active at dusk and at dawn.
Their keen sense of hearing keeps them ever aware;
Get too close - in a flash they'll be gone.

When disturbed this big hare will run like the wind
And reach forty per with such ease.
He'll leap three feet high and look 'round and grin.
It's called "spy-hopping" as he cuts through the breeze.

One jack rabbit is famous and has been for years.
His antics are always quite funny.
With his powder puff tail and extra long ears,
We know him by name – he's Bugs Bunny.

The Black Tailed Prairie Dog

Cynomys ludovicianus gives your tongue a good twist
It's a joke some mad scientist couldn't resist.
It's less of a dog and more of a squirrel,
The jokes just keep coming – my mind's in a twirl.

It ranges from Texas up through the Dakotas.
Most ranchers argue we've exceeded the quotas.
"They eat up the grasses, poke holes in the ground;
They ruin the pastures – a mess by the pound."

They actually help by reducing compaction
Of soil when the cattle are fighting for traction.
Their towns are preferred by all species grazing,
But ranchers don't buy it and continue their hazing.

The dogs (really squirrels) live on the Great Plains,
Far out on the prairie where seldom it rains.
The prairie dog towns once covered vast spaces,
But now can be found in just certain places.

The towns, like our cities, display subdivisions,
With neighborhoods having their zoning provisions.
A coterie's made of a male and his mates.
They'll keep out the neighbors without walls or gates.

The dogs burrow down from three to ten feet,
Then level it off, their home to complete.
The chambers, grass lined, are where the dogs nest,
But one special chamber's for when they must "rest."

The mouth of the tunnel has dirt all piled up.
It's like a volcano, but doesn't erupt.
Water can't get past the burrow's front hump;
A clever design since they have no sump pump.

Their porch is for visiting, gossiping, too.
They sit on their haunches, enjoying the view.
They still keep a vigil for coyotes and hawks
And any big critter that crawls, flies or walks.

(Continued)

They eat all the foliage around the front mound.
This makes for poor hiding, a strategy sound.
With danger detected, a chirp and a wheeze;
All vanish so fast that they kick up a breeze.

When danger has passed, there's yipping and jumping,
Then all will emerge with little fists pumping.
They fight with each other, all rivals, bar none,
But with predators lurking, they function as one.

Blue Grama

Bouteloua gracilis, Blue Grama as it's known,
Makes the Great Plains its primary home.
It's ninety percent of the prairie short grass,
Which makes it the primary grass in that class.

It grows from six to twelve inches in height.
It's gray-green in appearance, at least in most light.
The flowers, like crescent moons, are perched on the stems;
From these come the seeds, prairie grass gems.

It's readily established and grows well from seed,
But relies most on tillers to spread like a weed.
Wind scatters the seeds, but only a few feet,
While disbursal by animals just can't be beat.

Blue grama grows best when planted alone,
So the competing plants don't dry the root zone.
The seeds, by themselves, won't send out new shoots,
But given some moisture, they send down their roots.

The plant can withstand heavy grazing and cold.
It's also drought tolerant; it goes dormant, on hold.
It's valued as forage and erosion control.
If it weren't for blue grama, we'd repeat the Dust Bowl.

The Bobcat

Felis rufus is the secretive Bobcat.
Rarely you'll see him, except for his scat.
With each encounter, you'll get such a rush,
But all that you'll see is his tail through the brush.

They're tan to gray-brown with some streaks of black.
They blend with the foliage when set to attack.
Its short tail looks "bobbed," which some people claim
Is how the bobcat was given its name.

They've adapted to swampland to arid and dry.
They'll live near the cities, although they're quite shy.
Their home range will vary, depending on season.
The males will range farther for obvious reasons.

Both sexes are loners, but meet up to mate.
Together they stay just to procreate.
In raising the young, the male has no role;
He mates with the female and then goes off on a stroll.

A litter is made up of two to four kittens.
They're so very cute, you'll surely be smitten.
They open their eyes at nine days or ten
And soon they are ready to emerge from the den.

Mom teaches them hunting skills until the next year.
By then they'll be able to bring down a deer.
They eat most small mammals and an occasional bird,
But will sometimes take poultry or young from a herd.

The bobcat's main threat, as usual, is man.
Hunting and autos reduce their life span.
I regret that mankind has not been a good keeper,
But serving instead as Nature's Grim Reaper.

The Boxelder

Acer negundo is the Boxelder tree;
The maples are very close kin.
It's an interesting tree, I think you'll agree,
When your study of this tree begins.

The leaves are opposite and pinnately compound,
With five, often seven leaflets.
You'll find that the leaves will sometimes confound
By resembling a plant of regrets.

The leaves of seedlings and less prosperous trees
Will often show leaflets of three.
They're often mistaken for poison ivy,
But instead of a shrub it's a tree!

It's a dioecious plant, each tree is one sexed,
That grows up to sixty feet tall.
The pollen from one will float to the next
Yielding samaras, the seeds, in the fall.

Samaras are seeds with a prominent wing,
Small "choppers" to delight a small child.
They spin to the ground in late fall or spring,
A method so elegantly styled.

You'll find the Boxelder throughout our great state,
But it's generally considered a weed.
Boxelder bug and decay are its fate,
But it grows well when most trees won't succeed.

The Brown Recluse

Loxosceles reclusa is the Brown Recluse spider,
Which refers to its color and habit.
If Miss Muffett had one of these sit down beside her,
I'm sure she would outrun a rabbit.

They're indigenous to the central Midwest
And south to the Dixieland shores.
They're frequently found as an unwanted guest
In undisturbed places indoors.

You'll find them in basements, ducts and crawl spaces,
Wherever the rascals might choose.
They'll also seek shelter in dangerous places,
Like clothes, bed linen and shoes.

This arachnid's thorax shows a dark violin,
Which gives this spider its flair.
Its fairly long legs are spindly and thin
And covered with very fine hair.

It roams in the dark searching for prey
Or for insects that are already dead.
Any old bug seems to be on its buffet.
It will enjoy what is on the night's spread.

They can move very fast, but they're somewhat inept,
They'll fall when they get near a brink.
You'll find in the morning, that while you've slept,
They've been trapped in the bathtub or sink.

Controlling these critters can take a long time;
Our tolerance is low for this pest.
A four pronged approach is thought to be prime
And will yield the results that are best.

Keep them outside by caulking all cracks
And get rid of old clothes, trash and clutter.
Vacuum, set traps and clean to the max
And spread pesticide as though it were butter.

This spider will bite when handled or crushed,
But they really are not all that hostile.
So tell your teenager, just don't get too rushed,
Shake clothes out when picked off that pile.

Buffalo Grass

Buchloe dactyloides, known as Buffalo Grass,
Is quite the epitome of prairie short grass.
It's forage for bison, pronghorn and deer,
And all grazing mammals, both far and near.

A blue-green perennial half a foot high,
It grows in most climates, but much prefers dry.
It easily withstands the heat, drought and cold.
Unlike modern grasses, it's unusually bold.

It often grows better just after a fire,
When dead leaves burn off so green leaves grow higher.
The soil has protected the plant from the heat.
While incongruous, it's a remarkable feat.

The plant will spread out from six to twelve feet
And form a dense carpet that's just hard to beat.
It's blue-green in summer, lavender in fall;
In cold winds of winter, there's no color at all.

To five feet in depth the thin roots can grow,
But most are quite shallow; to plows it's a foe.
The root system forms a sod very dense.
It makes a snug house and an ugly mud fence.

It seems almost perfect in lawns to be sown;
It wouldn't need water and wouldn't need mown.
It's too bad the grass has a delicate blade
That won't withstand traffic and doesn't like shade.

The Bullsnake

Pituophis catenifer sayi is the Bullsnake of the prairie,
A magnificent snake, to be sure.
Some are quite docile, but some are contrary;
Be careful - resist their allure.

He'll have rather dark markings on honey-brown hide,
With a belly that's light brownish-yellow.
His body is heavy, bulky and wide,
And at five feet, he's a formidable fellow.

He seems to have a perpetual glare
From scales overhanging each eye.
His rostral (nose) scale has additional flare;
It seems it's gone somewhat awry.

Like most other snakes, his forked tongue is used
To pick up the scent of his prey.
He'll detect the essence that's been diffused
In the air and wafted his way.

On many small mammals the Bullsnake will feed,
Which is their primary ecological role.
They silently slip through the timber and weeds
Scouting burrows, like prairie dog holes.

The bullsnake is surely another constrictor
Who wraps around his quarry, so tight.
He squeezes until he's proclaimed the victor
And his prey just no longer can fight.

This snake will frequently thermoregulate
On a roadway beneath sunny sky.
He'll often, quite sadly, meet up with his fate.
When a speeding vehicle comes by.

This snake can produce a very loud hiss
And posture as though it will strike.
It's trying to tell you that things are amiss,
So keep walking and continue your hike.

The Canada Goose

Branta canadensis is the Canada Goose.
We now have so many, they're trouble on the loose.
They're found near the water where it's open and grassy,
But on golf links and airports, they can get very sassy.

They're generally gray, very elegant chaps,
With black necks and heads and milky chin straps.
They're light underneath with very black feet
And one of the handsomest birds that you'll meet.

Teeth-like lamellae 'round the edge of their bills
Surely assist with their foraging skills.
They're used as a cutting tool for the various grasses
Which are gobbled by geese that are eating in masses.

They never fly behind or beside one another,
But are staggered just back, each from the other.
This reduces the drag and allows them to use
The slipstream of birds just ahead in the cruise.

The geese, therefore, fly in a big V formation,
With birds taking turns in the primary station.
They migrate at a slow pace and stop on the way
So they arrive in good shape with no physical decay.

They're monogamous birds, both husband and wife;
They're together for years, and even for life.
Mom incubates eggs in the nest that she built,
While dad defends all while showing no guilt.

They become quite obnoxious when they stay all year round.
They overgraze lawns and leave dung by the pound.
They'll damage the crops and pollute the water.
Some think the best cure is a widespread goose slaughter.

The Canada Goose is a magnificent bird,
Whether aloft in formation or afoot in a herd.
You can't help but watch them when they are on wing;
They totally captivate and make your heart sing.

The Cicada

Several species of insect, Cicadas as they're known,
Share one common feature: their deafening drone.
With prominent eyes and transparent wings
And at two inches long, they're our insect kings.

All have tympana, equivalent of ears,
So they can hear sounds, or so it appears.
The males have the noisemakers, tymbals, they're called,
And can reach many decibels, loudest insect of all.

The tymbal's a membrane that's vibrated with ease
By using strong muscles, which relax and then squeeze.
Large tracheal chambers resonate the sound
Producing the noise for which they're renowned.

The cicada lays eggs in some slits in a twig.
The newly hatched nymphs hit the ground for a dig.
Depending on species, the underground scene
Will vary from two years up to seventeen.

The nymphs feed on root juice and burrow around
From one foot to eight feet deep in the ground.
In the final nymphal instar, they come up through the grass
To molt one more time; they're adults, at long last.

The *Magicicadas* will emerge in a brood
And are quite recognizable, I'm sure you'll conclude.
They're black with red eyes, with orange legs and wings.
They show up each thirteen or seventeen springs.

The *Tibicens* are larger and come up each year.
They're green, black or brown with wings that are clear.
When either emerges, you'll instantly know.
You'll hear their incessant, weeee-oh, weeee-oh.

The Common Nighthawk

Chordeiles minor is the Common Nighthawk.
It's really a nightjar, not close to a hawk.
It nabs insects in flight with bristles 'round its bill
Just like its close cousin, the whip-poor-will.

It has white bars on wings and another on tail,
Beige throat on the female, but white on the male.
It has long pointed wings and an extended forked tail.
You'll know it at once; you just cannot fail.

It nests on bare ground or places just burned.
In cities, flat gravel roofs are never spurned.
Two eggs are usually laid flat on the ground,
In hopes that by predators the nest won't be found.

Open woodlands and fields are where they'll be found,
But they also have moved into cities and towns.
Athletic fields, with all of the lights,
Raise the hunting of insects to marvelous heights.

They hunt from near sundown on through to sunrise
Catching grasshoppers, moths, mosquitoes and flies.
They're often called bullbats because of their flight
And the fact that they're hunting at dusk and at night.

The nighthawk's a misnomer, from the word go.
Neither strictly nocturnal, nor is hawk apropos.
Nor should *Chordeiles **minor*** cause you to balk,
Because it is larger than the Lesser Nighthawk.

The Copperhead
(Appendix C)

Agkistrodon contortrix laticinctus is our copperhead snake.
It lives in the timber near pond, stream or lake.
It's kin to the cottonmouth, but not near as deadly.
It's reclusive, nocturnal, but will still bite you readily.

They're tan and light brown; variations are many,
But the ones found in Kansas are like a bright penny.
They're really quite pretty, when recently shed,
And searching for rodents in your flower bed.

They're ovoviparous, give birth to live young;
Up to eight babies with flicking forked tongue.
Their venom and fangs are ready to go,
So when prey wanders by, a bite they'll bestow.

The juveniles have a bright, green-yellow tail
To entice little insects and prey they can nail.
The tail fades to brown within the first year.
By then the snake ambushes prey that comes near.

They'll rarely be longer than a couple of feet,
And less toxic than most pit vipers you'll meet.
The bite's rarely fatal, but causes great pain.
You'll surely decide not to hold them again.

They're very well camoed when found in the timber.
They'll be close at hand, so you'd better be limber.
While very tenacious with a belligerent tone;
You'll be well advised just to leave them alone.

The Cottonwood

Populous deltoides, subspecies *sargentii,*
Towers o'er the prairie, contrasts the blue sky.
At ninety feet tall, to heaven it reaches
Exposes our frailty; humility teaches.

It's distinguished by thick and deep fissured bark,
Some of it light gray, some of it dark.
The diamond shaped leaves with odd petioles
Flutter and tremble when the wind rolls.

The sexes are separate, dioecious, you know;
When males give off pollen, the females yield snow.
This snow is the cotton that carries the seeds
To far away places on ethereal steeds.

Leaves, alternate, simple and coarsely serrated
Are triangle shaped, thus *deltoides* created.
A riparian species, it grows near some water.
Without these big fellows, this place would be hotter.

The cottonwood's regal; it's both wide and tall.
It sings in the summer; it's resplendent in fall.
It grows on the prairie, entwined with our fate,
Thus it's the recognized tree of our state.

The Coyote

The wily coyote is *Canis latrans.*
It means "barking dog," "prairie wolf" to his fans.
They're found on this continent, from Panama north.
From one common ancestor did canines come forth.

The coyote will stand up to two feet in height,
With fur that can range from tan to gray-white.
His big bushy tail is carried low to the ground;
A trait that's distinctive, for which he's renowned.

While not underfed, he appears very lean.
With a scowl on his face, he also looks mean.
His head seems too small for his nose and big ears,
But with great acuity he smells and he hears.

The coyote will mate and give up his heart
And stand by his lady till death do them part.
Four to six pups will whelp in a year.
To be raised by the parents and a few older peers.

The coyote will call, to some they will sing,
But mostly you'll hear them in the fall and the spring.
The call is a howl with succeeding short notes
And fills the night air from deep in their throats.

They'll hunt after dark and enjoy Nature's mart
And alter their diet to dine ala carte.
Rabbits and squirrels, voles, veggies and mice,
Whatever turns up with the roll of the dice.

The claims made by ranchers are very pretentious,
So the killing of coyotes is still quite contentious.
In spite of the hunting and coyote control,
They're thriving and doing quite well, on the whole.

They've adapted to living in city and park.
They sleep in the day and prowl in the dark.
They're thriving in spite of man's boundless intrusion.
If you think you have seen one, it's not an illusion.

The Deer Tick

Ixodes scapularis is the infamous Deer Tick,
An important vector of disease.
In many locales, they can be very thick
In the grasses, the bushes and weeds.

The ticks rest themselves at the top of a blade
To wait for a host to pass by.
They'll hitch a ride as you walk through the glade,
For their nourishment on you they rely.

Their mouth area has a harpoon-like feature
To anchor them firmly in place.
This hypostome fixes them to the poor creature
And gives them a lasting embrace.

The larva attaches to a mammal or bird
And gorges on blood for a time.
If this host is infected, the spirochete is conferred,
Now the tick spreads the disease known as Lyme.

The larva becomes a nymph after molting
And lays dormant until the next spring.
The nymph catches hold of a host that is bolting
And on that new host it will cling.

The nymph is the size of a small poppy seed.
Until it's engorged, it's not noticed.
It stays on the host to suck and to feed,
Especially when its site is remotest.

The nymph then drops off and molts once again
To become the mature, adult tick.
They'll catch a new host as it walks through the glen
To continue its life-cycle schtick.

The adult ticks will mate, with a courtship crusade;
This is their last major mission.
Around three thousand eggs by the female will be laid,
Then she dies having fulfilled life's ambition.

Ticks spread diseases, but don't act psychotic,
'Cause most are relatively rare.
All can be treated with antibiotics,
So with ticks, you should just be aware.

The Eastern Cottontail

Silvilagus floridanus is our cute cottontail.
You'll find them in cities and o'er hill and dale.
You'll find them in parks and in your back yard;
To find where they aren't is exceedingly hard.

The female can breed at three months of age.
That seems very young, but is certainly sage.
The altricial young (they require much care),
Are small, quite defenseless, and without any hair.

Two to four litters are produced every year,
With six to eight bunnies per litter, oh dear!
If not for predation, their numbers would creep;
We'd be covered in rabbits, scores of feet deep.

They're cute little bunnies when munching on clover,
But are all bleepin' rabbits when the garden's run over.
They'll eat up your cabbage and carrots and greens,
Tomatoes and turnips and just sprouted beans.

They're preyed on by bobcats, foxes and birds.
Our thanks to them cannot be put into words.
Rabbits are cute, but too often a pest.
When not in my yard, I like them the best.

The Eastern Hognose Snake

Heterodon platirhinos is the Eastern Hognose,
A very interesting critter.
He'll act quite aggressive in menacing shows
But you'll find that he's really a quitter.

He'll posture and coil, vomit and flail,
And act in a manner quite brusque.
He'll be covered in feces from his head to his tail,
As well as with foul smelling musk.

He'll hiss and he'll lunge and his hood will be spread,
To convince you that he's very tough.
Then he'll convulse, roll over and play dead
When it's clear his display's not enough.

They vary in color from tan to dark gray,
With blotches which lead to mistakes.
These alternate blotches will form an array.
That resembles the fierce rattlesnakes.

With their very conspicuous, upturned snout,
They burrow in loose soil with ease.
They'll push the loose soil around and about
With great serpentine expertise.

The hognose is specialized for eating a toad,
Even when it's fully inflated.
Its jaws have been especially bestowed
So that they can be greatly dilated.

The Hognose produces protective hormones
To help deal with toxic secretions.
Their special saliva has also been shown
To subdue the hapless amphibians.

The Eastern Hognose is truly unique,
But its numbers continue to erode.
It's too bad its future appears to be bleak
But it follows the loss of the toad.

The Eastern Redbud

Cercis canadensis is the Redbud in spring,
Which adds color when all else is gray.
You know that Ol' Winter has taken to wing
And warm weather is not far away.

The blossoms erupt in a lavender show
Before the leaves can appear.
As soon as the heart-shaped leaves say "hello,"
The spectacle's gone till next year.

They're frequently found in that transition zone
'tween timber and prairie, or lea.
They typically grow where the sunlight has shown,
Just not directly under a tree.

It likes partial shade, but will grow in full light,
So it's valued as an ornamental.
It grows to a modest five meters in height,
But its shape can be detrimental.

The tree is often unbalanced in form
And frequently leans with old age.
I guess that the redbud just follows the norm
And gets feeble in life's latter stage.

The Eastern Red Cedar

Juniperus virginiana has garnered ill fame.
It's really a juniper, but cedar by name.
It sprouts in the fence rows and long fallow fields.
It looks quite innocuous, but damage it deals.

A slow growing tree, it's hardy and hale;
The "grave yard tree" from an old woman's tale.
A young man will plant one. By the time that he dies,
It'll shade his poor grave and keep sun from his eyes.

Moths will avoid the wood's fragrant smell.
The tree makes good pencils and longbows, as well.
The little blue balls on the branches are seeds,
And they satisfy many birds' caloric needs.

Seeds, gobbled down, are quickly ingested
And pass through the bird without being digested.
Birds eat the seeds while branch to branch hopping,
Then scatter them widely along with their dropping.

It grows where not wanted, it's range pioneered.
It squats in land damaged or recently cleared.
It doesn't like forests, but delights in the sun.
When it gains the least foothold, survival is won.

By growing in fields, it gives a nice perch
To raptors and prey birds, from where they can lurch.
The number of game birds will certainly fall,
So it's best if the fields have no cedars at all.

The Flameleaf Sumac

Rhus copallina, the Flameleaf Sumac,
Has so many names, you'll be taken aback.
Flameleaf or winged, dwarf sumac or shining,
The plant is the same, just the name's not confining.

A deciduous shrub up to two meters in height,
It grows on the prairie in thickets, so tight.
The leaves are alternate, pinnately compound;
They're bright red in the fall, for which they're renowned.

There isn't a soil that won't make its day,
From acid to basic and sandy to clay.
Dry soil and full sun make a home worth pursuing.
Neither drought nor strong winds will be its undoing.

"Sumac" and "poison" are connected, I'll grant,
But *copallina*'s not poison, like some other *Rhus* plants.
The sumac, *Rhus vernix*, will give you remorse,
As will *toxicodendron,* the ivy, of course.

It's said that the plant has medicinal uses,
From root, stem and leaves to the fruit and its juices.
For VD and dysentery and dermal eruptions,
It's rumored that sumac will ease these corruptions.

The thickets give shelter to much wildlife,
And offer protection from their daily strife.
The plant is quite common throughout the Great Plains,
So enjoy it while driving down highways and lanes.

The Fox Squirrel
(Appendix D)

Sciurus niger is the squirrel tinted red,
Who much prefers oak-hickory grounds.
Sciurus carolinensis is the color of lead
And tends to reside in the towns.

Both squirrels will forage for food on the ground
Or eat seeds and buds in the trees.
They'll scamper between or from tree to tree bound,
And do both with the greatest of ease.

They often cache nuts, acorns and such,
In shallow holes hither and yon.
For dispersal of seeds, the trees rely much
On the squirrels' habits and brawn.

The squirrel is wary and streaks to a tree
When threatened by man or by beast.
To the opposite side of the tree he will flee,
Like lightening that's heavily greased.

Their home is usually a ball of dried leaves
Perched high in a trees upper boughs.
But it could be a hole in your own dwellings eaves
Or wherever his fortune allows.

January and June are when mating occurs,
With "mating chases" commonly seen.
A few ardent "hims" will pursue just one "her,"
Each vying to make her his queen.

In just six short weeks, she'll have several kits,
Who will be foraging in forty five days.
They'll be on your house and giving you fits
From sun-up till evening's last rays.

Some people call squirrels tree rats,
While others will call them much worse.
When they chew up your house to build cozy flats,
You'll be ready to call them a hearse.

The Garden Spider
(Appendix E)

Argiope aurantia is the Garden Spider, black and yellow,
That's in a class known as orb-weaver.
If you think this spider's a bland little fellow,
You just aren't a true believer.

The female is much larger than the male,
But together they're a beautiful pair.
With bodies alike to the smallest detail
And cephalothoraxes covered with fine silver hair.

The male communicates with his mate
By plucking or vibrating her net.
He'll live on the edge of her larger estate
And be ready for young to beget.

They have three claws on each of their feet
To help handle the threads while they're spinning.
This feature puts them in the spider elite,
Building elegant webs from the beginning.

The silk can be varied into seven diverse kinds
By changing the silk composition.
They can make silken traps or structural lines,
By using their own volition.

The web is constructed by emitting a thread
That drifts until touching an object.
She then adds more lines to her aerial bed,
Her bug-catching net to perfect.

The female will spin a web spiraling out
From the center to a very large size.
She'll spin her large web in an often used route
To catch insects and filter the skies.

The spiraling threads will remain very sticky,
'Cause these threads actually catch prey.
Now she is ready, albeit quite tricky,
For insects to attend her soiree.

(Continued)

A vertical zig-zag can often be seen
In the midst of the webs larger scheme.
This stabilimentum steadies the screen
And enhances the geometric theme.

On a damp early morning, strung between stems,
It's truly a magnificent view
To find this huge web all laden with gems;
Hundreds of droplets of dew.

The Grasshopper

Dissosteira carolina is the common grasshopper.
It starts out quite small, but grows into a whopper.
Three to four inches is the span of their wings.
They're large and abundant; they're grasshopper kings.

They're found in all of the forty-eight states,
Identified by their wing banding traits.
They live in the grasslands and weedy fence rows,
Along roadsides and railways; whenever one goes.

Successive instars occur as it ages.
They molt and grow larger in each of these stages.
They're active in daylight and seek shelter by night.
They're really quite wary and quick to take flight.

They'll eat what's on hand, their diets will vary
To include all the plants which grow on the prairie.
They'll eat every bite, be it brome grass or clover;
They'll eat every morsel with nothing left over.

They're voracious feeders because of their size,
And sometimes form swarms that will darken the skies.
They'll swoop down on farms and eat up the crops.
They'll defy every tactic till each farmer drops.

The grasshopper makes a good eating machine,
Its efficiency borders upon the obscene.
The last living thing on the earth, it's agreed,
Will be a grasshopper upon a dead weed.

The Great Blue Heron

Ardea herodias wardii
Is the Great Blue Heron in our state
His voice is very distinctive
And on your nerves it will grate.
Ardea, in Latin means heron,
Herodias is heron to Greeks.
Whatever the language you use,
You'll know him as soon as he speaks.

Blue herons will live near the water,
Like a river, a marsh or a lake.
They nest in the bushes and trees close at hand,
About that there is no mistake.
They're the largest of herons around;
They stand 'bout a meter in height.
They have beautiful gray upper bodies
With necks streaked with black, brown and white.

The males are larger than females
And display a black, puffy plume.
They're monogamous breeders each year;
For a harem, there just isn't room.
Up to seven blue eggs form a clutch,
With Big Daddy taking his turns
To sit on the eggs in the nest,
Allaying the mothers concerns.

They'll live to the ripe age of fifteen,
Perhaps a little bit more,
But most of the chicks will die by year one
Or maybe a few months before.
They hunt by themselves in the morning
And hunt again in the dusk.
They'll pugnaciously defend their home grounds
And speak in a manner quite brusque.

Their diet is made up of fish
Or anything else in the water.
They use their sharp bills to catch all their food;
It's just a veritable slaughter.
They're preyed on by eagles and hawks,
By raccoons and vultures and others.
They'll abandon their nest and area
If a predator kills one of their brothers.

(Continued)

The blue heron is called a blue crane,
Long john or poor joe as a prank.
He's also referred to as Big Cranky,
I guess, 'cause his call sounds like kraaank.
The heron's a beautiful bird;
A pleasure to watch while he wades.
The problem is that he's so wary,
You'll just watch as his silhouette fades.

The Great Horned Owl

Bubo virginianus is the Great Horned Owl.
Like most of this group, it was born with a scowl.
From the arctic clear down to the Magellan Straits,
You'll know it at once by its most prominent traits.

This very large bird with ear tufts on its head
Will send chills up your back and fill you with dread.
Its soft and loose feathers allow silent flight;
They'll scare you to death, when hiking at night.

Like all other birds, the owl has four toes,
But can shift one about so that two toes oppose.
A strong grip on a limb is what this trait permits
And transforms the talons into good "catcher's mitts."

Owls see in the daytime; they're surely not blind,
But their prey is nocturnal, so their skills are refined.
With near silent flight and excellent night vision,
They swoop down on prey with amazing precision.

They eat mostly mammals, like rabbits and mice,
But will eat ducks and game birds and never think twice.
They'll eat it all down; just eat like a zealot,
Then spit up the bad parts in the form of a pellet.

Love songs are sung between female and beau,
Then they use an old nest from a hawk or a crow.
They're very protective; the owlets are blessed.
They'll guard their young family till they leave the nest.

You'll hear different sounds when the Great Horned owl speaks,
From deep booming hoots to hair-raising shrieks.
It may give you a start, but don't be beguiled;
Its voice is a classical call of the wild.

The Greater Prairie Chicken

Tympanuchus cupido is the Greater Prairie Chicken.
When hunting at dusk, they'll make your heart quicken.
You think that you've sat in the ideal position,
Then they stay out of range through some intuition.

The name is descriptive for this bird that's so wary:
It's as big as a chicken and lives on the prairie.
It's also been called the "pinnated grouse"
For the tuft of neck feathers used to woo a young spouse.

The bird's strongly barred with white, tan and brown,
With legs that are feathered from the thigh clear on down.
The male will display his orange colored air sacs,
When he's fully engaged in his bold courtship acts.

The males will display on booming grounds, or leks,
While fluffing their pennae on the sides of their necks.
They inflate their air sacs and snap their short tails.
When hens come to watch, the best dancer prevails.

Prairie chickens don't migrate; they stay close to home.
They will travel for food, if they have to roam.
They eat mostly soy beans, milo and corn
Left on the ground 'neath the cornucopia horn.

The chickens require some native vegetation
To maintain their lifestyle and a strong population.
Conversion to farming leads to their demise;
If the trend's not reversed, you can say your good-byes.

The Green Darner Dragonfly

Anax junius is the Green Darner Dragonfly,
But it's not fully green, as the name would imply.
They'll have a green thorax, that much is true,
But their abdomens are garnet, tinged with light blue.

They much prefer water that's tranquil or static
With few hungry fish, but much foliage aquatic.
They typically capture small insects with ease,
Like midges and flies and mosquitoes and bees.

The males will compete to decide mating rights
By racing or dueling in aerial fights.
A mating wheel is formed by the amorous mates
So sperm can be transferred when they procreate.

The eggs will be laid at the edge of the ponds,
In old rotting wood or in weeds' many fronds.
The eggs will hatch out with nymphs as results.
They'll take several years to grow into adults.

The adult dragonfly is a very strong flyer
And can zip back and forth, not seeming to tire.
In straightaway flight, they can reach eighteen per,
Which is fast for an insect, I think you'll concur.

With translucent wings and large bulbous eyes,
The Green Darner dragonfly is easy to spy.
As always, its habitat loss that's the danger,
Which will make the Green Darner a summertime stranger.

The Honey Locust

Gleditsia triacanthos is the venerable Honey Locust.
It's a native, fast-growing tree.
Whenever you're near it, you'd better stay focused
Or you'll regret it, I guarantee.

This locust grows thorns up to eight inches long.
To climb it, you'll surely get flustered.
They'll be single or branched with multiple prongs
Or, more commonly, quite densely clustered.

The leaves are usually pinnately compound,
With leaflets about an inch long.
It displays a fairly loosely packed crown,
So the shade is moderate, not strong.

Bees don't make honey from this locust tree;
It's the pulp from the pods that is sweet.
The tree's a legume, like the peanut or pea,
Which horses and cattle will eat.

Enzymes will help to digest the seed coat,
Which facilitates seed germination.
In this way, the livestock is used to promote
The locust's dissemination.

The pods could be used to make a crude beer;
The thorns took the place of steel nails.
You had to make do when on the frontier,
To keep going when everything fails.

According to legend, the Thunder Spirit's son
Could sit on these branches with ease.
Only a spirit would not be undone
To climb up and sit in these trees.

The Ivy-Leaved Morning Glory

Ipomoea hederacea, the Ivy-Leaved Morning Glory,
Is a beautiful plant, which has its own story.
It's an annual vine, up to six feet in length
And twines around things with remarkable strength.

The alternate leaves are four inches by four
And are deeply three lobed; you couldn't want more.
Smooth margins are wavy, like an erratic fairy,
While the leaves upper surfaces are more or less hairy.

The flowers are funnelform, two inches across.
To find one more beautiful, you'd be at a loss.
They're shades of bright blue, through purple to pink,
Which attracts bumblebees, for pollination, I think.

The flower is supplanted by a pod with three cells.
Four to six seeds within each pod will dwell.
Pheasants and quail will devour the seeds,
But for most other birds, they won't meet their needs.

They bloom in morning on bright sunny days,
But will cover their heads without Ol' Sols rays.
Like us, they will meet a bright day with a "howdy,"
But would rather sleep in when it's rainy or cloudy.

The Jayhawk

Jayhawkornis kansasensis is a quarrelsome bird.
If you think it is quiet, you just haven't heard.
As part sparrow hawk, the balance blue jay,
It will upset tranquility and ruin your day.

Hesperornis regalis was the Jayhawk's grandpappy;
A cretaceous avian who dressed very snappy.
It had regal stature at five feet in height,
And a beak full of teeth, so beware of its bite.

The Jayhawk's a Phoenix; Assyrians it haunted.
It rose from the ashes and brimstone undaunted.
When Quantrill came raiding and Lawrence was burned,
The townsfolk, defiant, to Phoenix they turned.

The Jayhawks fought Redlegs from over the border,
But finally won out and restored civil order.
The Jayhawks made Kansas another Free State.
To fight for man's freedom, it's never too late.

Jayhawks are immortal and their battles of old
Give way to new struggles, equally bold.
'Gainst Wildcats and Tigers and Husker's Red Hoard,
Sooners and Tarheels and Blue Devils, Oh, Lord!

Rock Chalk, Jayhawk is the chant of the school.
It's known 'round the world because it's so cool.
Our mascot is famous, alone in its class.
It walks with a strut just exuding its sass.

Jayhawks are early birds, oldest of terms.
Still they have caught many Mizz-ery worms.
They're proud; they're defiant and cannot be faulted.
They simply refuse to have their tails salted.

The Jayhawk

His head is all crimson and his body bright blue
And his large yellow beak has a great smile for you.
He has a square buckle on each yellow shoe;
His chest is puffed out 'cause it's sportin' **KU**

He walks with a strut; you just know that he's proud.
There's only one like him – he stands out in a crowd.
He's the envy of mascots from East coast to West.
They all fight for second; they know he's the best.

He's part sparrow hawk and the rest is blue jay
To say that he's feisty is almost cliché.
He wears those big shoes to stomp on his foes
And all interlopers who dare to oppose.

There are Wildcats and Tigers and other such critters,
But when they're around him, they all have the jitters.
Those felines get docile, each cowers and purrs;
They know if they don't, they'll feel his sharp spurs.

When they meet on the gridiron or Phog Allen's court,
They know that the Jayhawk will be a good sport.
They know he'll play hard, though their plans will be wrecked,
They'll always be given their share of respect.

It doesn't much matter how hard rivals work,
They'll never wipe off that smug Jayhawk smirk.
They're envious and jealous clear down to the bone
'Cause the Jayhawk is in a class of his own.

The Killdeer

Charadrius vociferous is the little Killdeer;
To see him each summer produces much cheer.
The killdeer is really a shorebird, a plover.
He'll nest anywhere, on rocks or in clover.

With brown back and wings, white belly and breast,
A black and white bib; they're exquisitely dressed.
They can run very fast on fairly long legs
To keep any danger away from their eggs.

If the killdeer suspects that her nest is in danger,
She'll put on an act to sidetrack the stranger.
She'll flop and she'll flap with feigned broken wing
And all through the act, a distress call she'll sing.

When the varmint's been decoyed away from the nest,
She "recovers" and flies away, mocking the pest.
It's really amusing to watch her display
And the look on the stranger - utter dismay.

Little Bluestem

Andropogon scoparius is the Little Bluestem;
A botanist's joke that's perpetuated by them.
It's mostly not blue and it's surely not small
And when it is blue, it's not noticed at all.

At five feet in height, it's just a "small" grass;
A very significant plant in its class.
It gives cover for critters and many small birds
And is excellent forage for buffalo herds.

It forms a dense sod all over the prairie
And keeps the rich soil from getting too "airy."
It holds down erosion from water and wind,
So topsoil stays home and farms needn't mend.

When explorers came up the Big Mo and the Kaw,
The American Desert is what they first saw.
A desert, indeed, 'cause they couldn't see
For all of the bluestem, even one single tree!

The Meadowlark

Sturnella neglecta, the bird I like best,
Has brown and black wings and bright yellow chest.
He sports a big bib that is shiny and black
And blends with the prairie, when seen from the back.

He sits on a fence post and sings through the day,
Hoping to lure a young lady his way.
Once a young hen to his melody clings,
He'll start puffing and hopping and flapping his wings.

After they've mated, she builds them a home;
A small wickiup, it's a grass covered dome.
It's always a hazard to nest on the ground;
Concealment is key so their home won't be found.

Three to six speckled eggs form the first clutch.
They hatch in twelve days; that's surely not much.
The youngsters soon fledge and move out on their own.
Survival depends on the skills that they hone.

The pair still has time to raise a new brood,
Providing there's water and plenty of food.
Six to twelve offspring from just one relation?
Many are lost to excessive predation.

The meadowlark now is the Kansas state bird.
His pure voice will still a discouraging word.
He sits on his fence post surveying the trail,
While some city slicker mistakes him for quail.

Mead's Milkweed

Asclepias meadii is the Mead's Milkweed.
The species is threatened, so we need to pay heed.
While not yet endangered, it's headed that way,
So let's keep its place in the eco-bouquet.

The tear-drop shaped leaves are attached to the stem.
There are two to six alternate pairs of them.
An umbrel's the flowers, one to a score,
Shaped like an umbrella pointed down to the floor.

The bumblebee embodies the milkweed's close mate.
Without it the plant would not cross pollinate.
The problem, in most sites - the plants are too few
To attract and make use of a pollination crew.

Even when in bloom they're hard to discover,
They blend in so well with the prairie grass cover.
In Kansas, Mead's can be found in a hundred locations,
Which represents most of the world population.

The Monarch Butterfly

Danaus plexippus is the Monarch Butterfly.
Its orange and black wings will capture your eye.
Their wings may have a four inch wide span,
When they're unfolded and spread like a fan.

When looking at milkweed, it is a delight
To find monarch eggs, small, spherical and white.
A black, white and yellow striped larva will hatch
To forage and grow on the host milkweed patch.

The larva devours the poisonous leaves
To take up the toxin, themselves to achieve
A poisonous aspect for birds that might prey
Upon them while they go fluttering away.

The larva next enters the key pupal stage
And forms a green chrysalis, to mature and age.
In a couple of weeks, the adult will emerge
To mate and continue the life cycle urge.

Some monarchs will migrate, a remarkable feat,
But it takes up to three generations to complete.
To Mexican mountains for two thousand miles,
Through all sorts of dangers, a myriad of trials.

The monarchs appear to be in decline
Which some people say is not a good sign.
Habitat loss is taking its toll,
From Mexican forest to milkweed control.

To reverse this trend, while begging their pardon,
We can replant the milkweed in a butterfly garden.
We can add to our knowledge of this beautiful beast
By joining in Monarch Watch; catch, tag and release.

The Muskrat
(Appendix F)

Ondatra zibethicus is the common muskrat.
It's much like a field mouse, but considerably fat.
From Gulf to far North, from east coast to west,
It has many attributes, but is sometimes a pest.

The muskrat is so called because on the male
There are glands to make musk, which gets spread on the trail.
He deposits the substance along travel routes
To mark off his space, wherever it suits.

They live in a marsh or slow moving stream,
Backwater of lakes; you see the theme.
It can't be so shallow as to freeze to the floor,
So most of the lodges are away from the shore.

The muskrat is covered with waterproof fur,
Which keeps it afloat, whenever astir.
The dense, silky underfur keeps it quite warm
In the ice covered water, which in winter is norm.

Specialized hair is found on the hind feet.
It functions as webbing so swimming is fleet.
The front paws are used like humans use hands,
To perform all the tasks that Nature demands.

The muskrat, like the beaver, has sharp chisel teeth
To harvest its food o'er water or 'neath.
Its lips close around them so he stays composed,
While gnawing submerged with his mouth tightly closed.

It eats mostly cattails, wild rice, willow limb,
But sometimes eats fish when pickings are slim.
Cattails are food, but used to build shelter;
The lodges are mounds with cattails askelter.

A typical lodge will have several ways in
And one central chamber, or nesting den.
Sometimes the mound is much more complex,
Much like an apartment or, at least, a duplex.

The muskrat is vicious when under attack.
It stands its ground fiercely with no escape track.
So many mammals look cuddly and cute,
But will cause you to bleed if you're not astute.

The Northern Bobwhite
(Appendix G)

Colinus virginianus is the Northern Bobwhite.
To hear them call out is a perpetual delight.
The name derives from their distinctive call;
The melodic "bob, bob white" just says it all.

They have a black cap and stripe past their eye;
If it's white in between, the bird is a guy.
Their body is brown with specks, black and white.
They blend with the foliage when they're sitting tight.

They usually walk, although they can fly.
They run very fast and are really quite spry.
When they are startled, they'll fly a short distance,
So hunting is best when a dog lends assistance.

Seeds and berries and mixed vegetation
Serve as the quail's winter diet foundation.
Whereas insects, snails, centipedes and spiders
Make up the summer's nutrition providers.

With a "hurt" wing, the bobwhite will feign,
To draw a predator from its nesting domain.
When the danger has passed, the bobwhite will scurry
Back to its nest in a brown feathered flurry.

The covey's a group that forms after mating.
Its primary use is in danger abating.
There's safety in numbers, so goes the old saying.
When the covey's together, it cuts down on preying.

When out hunting doves, you'll faint and go pale
When from under your feet flush a covey of quail.
Their wings beat so fast and make so much noise
That you'll drop your teeth and lose all your poise.

A crisp autumn morning with quail in the air
In many locales is becoming quite rare.
Management efforts are summed in three words;
Habitat, habitat, habitat will guarantee us these birds.

The Northern Water Snake
(Appendix H)

Nerodia sipedon is the Northern Water Snake,
A harmless denizen of the plains.
They'll be near some water, be it pond, creek or lake
Or any place water remains.

They have alternate blotches that run down their backs
Or they'll merge to form banded marks.
They vary in color from grayish to black,
With adults being totally dark.

The female will have just one litter per year,
Giving birth to dozens of young.
Once they are born, they disperse far and near,
While flicking their little forked tongues.

They're known both as scavenger and fierce carnivore;
They'll swallow whatever they find.
Snakes, fish and insects, frogs and much more,
Their tastes are hardly refined.

The Northern Water Snake is really a friend
And strengthens the fish population.
They cull out weak fish, which serves to extend
The fish's gene pool foundation.

They'll grow to a length of almost six feet,
Which makes them a subject of awe.
While more aggressive than most snakes you'll meet,
If you leave them alone they'll withdraw.

Unfortunately, this snake is too often killed
By people who are simply afraid.
They'll see "water moccasin" and their blood will be chilled,
Never knowing the mistake that they made.

The Cottonmouth, *Agkistrodon piscivorus,* can only be found
In Cherokee County, southeast.
So snakes throughout Kansas, that in water abound,
Should be respected, not harmed in the least.

The Opossum

Didelphis virginiana is the common Opossum.
There are societies of folks who think they're just awesome.
It's called a living fossil, it dates back so far.
It lived along side of the great dinosaur.

It's the only marsupial found in this vicinity.
To the koala and 'roo, there is quite close affinity.
The pouch yields *Didelphis*, which means double womb;
For infant opossums, it's their nursery room.

They're born just after ten or twelve days,
Then crawl to the pouch to spend their next phase.
Once in the pouch, they attach to a teat.
For the next couple months, they grow and they eat.

When the pouch gets too full, they ride on Mom's back,
But when ready to eat, they crawl back in the sack.
They'll ride on her back until they are grown
And able to make it out on their own.

You won't see them hang by their prehensile tail;
Their body's too heavy; the stunt would just fail.
Their tail is used for balance and grasp.
It wraps 'round a branch and forms a good clasp.

Playing possum is its defense to a threat
In hopes that the predator will leave and forget.
It enters a coma and lies in a lump.
With putrid, green fluid leaking out of its rump.

It can be ferocious; it can hiss and can shriek.
It's got fifty teeth and is surely not meek.
Just leave it alone and it'll go on its way
And you can relate how you've seen its display.

You'll commonly see them around your abode
Or lying quite still by the side of the road.
They'll eat insects or garbage or the family pet's food.
Or you can eat 'possum, roasted or stewed.

The Ornate Box Turtle

Terepene ornata, the Ornate Box Turtles,
May race the hares, but not in high hurdles.
They're five inches long and look like they're hand painted.
If you've lived here one summer, I'm sure you're acquainted.

Yellow dashes adorn its dark carapace,
From the top of its shell on down to the base.
The same yellow marks are on the plastron.
You'll know it at once when it's found in your lawn.

The male has red eyes, with leg scales to match
And a long, curved first claw for a nuptial clasp.
The female is lighter with brown head and eyes;
Very appealing to the dark, red eyed guys.

Growth rings are seen on each segment, or scute,
So you'll now know their sexes and ages, to boot.
The female is larger than a comparable brave
And you'll note that his plastron is slightly concave.

Two to eight eggs will be laid in a hole,
Then its traces wiped out, the female's last goal.
In a couple of months, the young will hatch out,
But may wait until spring 'fore wandering about.

When threatened, the turtle retreats into shell.
Its head, legs and tail are tucked in, as well.
The plastron is hinged and pulled up like a gate.
It stays all encased till the danger abates.

One thing you learned when you were a child,
When picking up turtles, was not to get riled.
You learned very quickly to hold them away
Or you would get wet from the turtle's dismay.

The Osage-Orange

Maclura pomifera, called many a name,
Whichever the moniker, the tree's still the same.
Mock- or osage-orange, hedge, or bois d'arc,
You'll find it surrounding a field or a park.

Planted in rows, ten meters in height,
They make a good fence, "horse high and hog tight."
Livestock stay in and trespassers out,
But keeping it trimmed is a championship bout.

The tree branch has spurs, mostly called thorns,
They're sharper than tacks and harder than horns.
The branches hang down as the tree grows in height;
Try to get through and you're in for a fight.

The fruit's like a softball, but bumpy and green.
Squirrels tear them apart like nothing you've seen.
They open them up to get at the seeds,
And sit on their haunches, so proud of their deeds.

The tree resists drought, wind, rot, vandals and storms.
It's ever so hardy; far exceeding the norms.
Used to make bows, Osage Indians were clever;
The things that they made from it lasted forever.

The tree is a beauty when grown out alone
And trimmed to stand upright, not puckered and prone.
With a crown that is broad and shade deep and dark,
A gnarled, twisted trunk and orange tinted bark.

The Oxeye Daisy

Chrysanthemum leucanthemum is the Oxeye Daisy.
In Scotland, they were called "gools."
This weed has spread through this country like crazy,
Because it won't follow the rules.

The flowers are approximately two inches wide,
Bright yellow surrounded by white.
The stems will be single, but sometimes divide,
And are one to three feet in height.

Each plant will produce thousands of seeds,
Which are viable for five to ten years.
This daisy is certainly one of those weeds,
Which bring farmers and ranchers to tears.

The oxeye will propagate well from its roots
And is resistant to most herbicides.
Cattle ignore and bypass the shoots,
Which just strengthens the oxeye weed's strides.

You'll find them in meadows and along side the roads
And on acreage that is going unsown.
The number of daisies will seem to explode
And the land will become overgrown.

There is no simple way to get rid of this pest;
Prevention is better than cure.
Multiple management methods are stressed
Like keeping your seed mixes pure.

Because oxeye is such a pretty wildflower,
Control is often neglected.
Ranchers must do everything in their power
To keep land from becoming infected.

Penstemon

Penstemon buckleyi is the pretty Penstemon.
In Kansas, you'll find it southwest.
From April to June, it won't be outdone,
For beauty, penstemon is blessed.

Flowers are lavender, pale pink or pale blue
With reddish-purple lines in the throat.
Flowers are many, eleven down to two,
Makes a thyrse that is worthy of note.

The Greek prefix, penta, means "five."
Five stamens give this plant acclaim.
From the one hairy stamen's contrived,
Beardtongue as its common name.

It's a herbacious perennial plant
That stands almost three feet in height.
When it's in blossom, I'll grant,
Penstemon's a beautiful sight.

The Prairie Coneflower

Ratibida columnifera is the Coneflower called the Mexican Hat.
It closely resembles a sombrero, at that.
The "crown" of brown disk florets is one inch in height,
While the five to ten "brim" florets are colored and bright.

Each alternate, pinnately divided leaf
Depicts a linear or lanceolate motif.
The leaves are quite large, six inches by three,
And appear stiffly hairy, to a certain degree.

The coneflower grows to a height of three feet.
In its early growth stage, cattle find it a treat.
It's resistant to drought and requires full sun.
To fill disturbed land, it is second to none.

Plains Indians made tea from the leaves and the flowers
And for rattlesnake bite the stems had great powers.
They used an infusion of the coneflower's top
To make their headaches and stomachaches stop.

Along highways and byways the coneflower grows
And out on the prairie where the wild wind blows.
In natural borders they add certain flair
And the best part of all, with almost no care.

Prairie Phlox

Phlox pilosa is the pretty Prairie Phlox.
Phlox in the Greek translates "flame."
From their brilliant bright red or their deep purple locks,
The phlox was given its name.

Pilosa will grow over two feet in height,
With one erect, branching stem.
The flowers are lavender, pink, rarely white,
With each plant having dozens of them.

It's found along roads, in meadows and leas
In the eastern part of the state.
Rhizomes permit it to sprout up with ease
To form clumps of phlox, so ornate.

It's a perennial plant from heavy rootstalk,
Flowering as late as July.
The lucky observer, when out for a walk,
Will find phlox a feast for the eye.

The Purple Coneflower

Echinacea purpurea is the Purple Coneflower.
The plant is long known for its medicinal power.
It was used to treat various ailments and pains
By the Indian tribes of the American plains.

Today it is used to improve one's immunity,
But isn't embraced by the medical community.
As with most herbals, there's varying purity
So therapy doesn't provide much security.

The coneflower's a perennial and tolerant of drought
It will grow in some shade, but prefers to be out.
At two to three feet, it's really quite stunning
In garden or field, while it sits there just sunning.

Its center appears like a rust colored cone,
Surrounded by florets in a lavender zone.
There're two types of flowers rolled into one,
Just like *Helianthus*, the "flower of the sun."

It's commercially grown for its medicinal yields,
And it's a very good plant for borders and fields.
Coneflowers will make Lepidoptera rejoice;
For a butterfly garden, it's an excellent choice.

The Raccoon

Procyon lotor is what we call a raccoon.
The word comes from Algonquian, *aroughcoune.*
Translated, it means "he who scratches with hands."
He has a mask on his face and a tail with black bands.

Extremely adaptable, they establish their nests
In moist woodland sites or become urban guests.
With thumb and four fingers, their paws are like hands,
And dexterous enough to thwart best laid plans.

They're intelligent omnivores, known to be clever.
They'll open a door with knob, latch or lever.
They're famous for being mischievous and sly;
They'll work to gain entry and never say die.

Nocturnal, omnivorous they sneak in like fairies
To eat insects or eggs, the trash or wild berries.
They often dowse food, get it soggy and wet,
But discerning the reason, we're not there quite yet.

Two to four young born each year to renew,
But most will not make it much beyond two.
The toll is to cars and hunter's night mission,
But many are lost simply to malnutrition.

They shuffle along, but can reach fifteen per.
They're also strong swimmers, but don't like wet fur.
They climb with agility, a bloodhound to stop;
Not bothered a bit by a forty foot drop.

Don't try to keep a raccoon for a pet.
It's hard to find help when they require a vet.
Their training becomes an ongoing chore;
Their natural behavior can be such a bore.

Raccoons will frequently harbor disease,
Like roundworm, distemper and, oh, yes, rabies.
It's best, when confronted, to keep well away;
Just call pest control to come save the day.

The Red Fox

Vulpes vulpes is the Red Fox so sly,
He can always outwit his foes.
No matter the tactics, he'll always defy,
At least in our poems and prose.

His body is slim and his legs are quite thin,
But his big tail is bushy and thick.
His large ears are pointed and so is his chin,
And his fur is the color of brick.

He's been hunted for fun and hunted for fur
And still, the red fox survives.
You'll find him wherever good pickings occur
And in spite of man's pressure, he thrives.

Whether urban or rural, they easily adapt,
And just carry on, at all cost.
They avoid many problems and never feel trapped
By habitat, shrinking or lost.

The omnivorous foxes will eat anything,
But subsist mostly on mice and on voles.
Like a cat, they capture their prey with a spring,
When the rodents emerge from their holes.

The majority of foxes never will mate,
And very few females will breed.
To help raise their siblings is often their fate;
To the family these foxes accede.

The vixen will have just one litter per year,
Which consists of three to four kits.
By eight weeks of age, they're exploring their sphere
And learning to live by their wits.

In old Aesop's fables the fox was depicted
As the model of cunning and guile.
The fox's intent could not be predicted
By trusting his actions and smile.

His eyes, like a cat, have vertical pupils,
Not rounded like all other canids.
With these evil eyes, he seems to lack scruples
In the forest when meeting lost kids.

The Red Oak

Quercus rubra is the majestic Red Oak
Of the eastern third of the state.
It adds to the autumn's magnificent cloak
With its beautiful red-orange pate.

It will grow to a height of seventy feet
And up to sixty feet wide.
It provides the squirrels a veritable treat
Of acorns they eat and they hide.

The acorn's a true nut, the botanist teaches,
Unlike the walnut or pecan.
They're really drupes, like cherries and peaches
Even with husks dried and gone.

The deeply lobed leaves are generally set
In an alternate pattern, or mien.
The leaves in the autumn are brick red, and yet,
In the summer they're shiny and green.

You'll find the red oak about anywhere,
But they grow best in moist fertile land.
In lawns, parks and links they are planted with care,
In line with a landscaping plan.

The red oak produces valuable wood;
In its grain pattern vast beauty lies.
Quarter-sawn oak is especially good
And such furniture makes excellent buys.

The Red-Tailed Hawk

Buteo jamaicensis, routine on the prairie,
Constructs a high nest, which is known as an aerie.
They build in tall trees or high up in rocks.
Wherever you go, you'll see red-tailed hawks.

The aerie is woven with large sticks and twigs,
And lined with fresh grasses and evergreen sprigs.
As many as four eggs the mother hawk lays.
They'll hatch in thirty to thirty-five days.

The youngsters will fledge in about seven weeks,
With sharp yellow eyes and sharper hooked beaks.
In three to four years they'll be soaring the skies,
With reddish-brown tails and reddish-brown eyes.

The hawk perches high and swoops down on its prey
Or patrols the wide prairie while soaring, by day.
They hold their wings steady in dihedral stance;
So prey isn't leery and won't look askance.

The hawk preys on rodents and mammalian pests,
But sometimes takes poultry in foraging quests.
The chickenhawk name is colloquially used,
But Red-Tail's protected, so seldom abused.

The hawk isn't picky when gathering meals.
Unwary critters are knocked on their heels.
Rabbits and pheasants and lizards and snakes,
Grouse, quail and catfish, whatever it takes.

The Red-Tail is common across this great land.
When man built the roads, it was given a hand.
The wide open roadways are good hunting spaces
And utility poles make superb nesting places.

It's great to sit idly and scan cloudless sky
To see splendid Red-Tails, with no effort they fly.
We watch them soar up from aerie in tree,
And imagine the feeling of being that free.

The Red-Winged Blackbird
(Appendix I)

Agelaius phoeniceus, the Red-Winged Blackbird,
Has a voice as distinctive as any you've heard.
Memories of fishing have stuck in my mind
With the gurgling "oak-a-lee" firmly entwined.

The male is all black with shoulders of red,
But can hide them and show yellow wing bands, instead.
The female is smaller with brown stripes so narrow
She could be mistaken for a very large sparrow.

Hayfields and swamps can be used when they nest,
But the freshwater marsh is the place they like best.
They feed upon insects, abundant in reeds,
But will also enjoy an assortment of seeds.

The red-wing is quite a polygynous bird
And the father of nestlings can surely get blurred.
One male can consort with a dozen plus hens,
But other young males will still breed with them.

At night they will congregate throughout the year,
But in winter the group gets much larger, it's clear.
A million black birds form this large group, alas,
With many bird species migrating en masse.

At sundown the birds seem to black out the sky,
As though the old king had just opened his pie.
A zillion black birds in a group is a shock.
It'd make a good movie for Alfred Hitchcock.

The Ring-Necked Pheasant

Phasianus colchicus is the Ring-Necked Pheasant.
It's used like a chicken when you bake.
When it's served under glass, the dining is pleasant,
But it won't take the place of my steak.

The pheasant's a bird with a very long tail;
It's about as long as its body.
As usual in birds, there's the elegant male,
With the female a cut above shoddy.

She's much less showy, mottled and brown,
With nothing that's worthy of note.
The cock is bedecked with a much brighter gown,
Notably, a white ring 'round his throat.

The rooster's a combo of russet and copper
And is covered with gray and black mottles.
His neck's shiny green and his head's black and proper,
Which shows off his brilliant red wattles.

They live on the grasslands, but like scrub and trees.
Such land will provide a nice diet.
With insects and seeds, they'll have life of ease.
Just don't knock it unless you will try it.

Like the quail, the pheasant's a short-distance flyer,
But much prefers a good run.
They can run through the grass and, it seems, never tire,
But can fly sixty per from your gun.

The male will mate with many a hen;
They never will form bonding pairs.
The male will "donate" to the female, and then
Leave her with the child raising cares.

The young are precocial and soon leave the nest;
They can fly in just a fortnight.
In this way, at least, the mother is blessed;
She's not long in the motherhood plight.

They're native to Asia, but before current laws,
Were introduced into the States.
The pheasants were welcomed with the hunter's applause
And the epicure's elegant plates.

The Sandhill Crane

Grus canadensis, the Sandhill Crane,
Is one of the largest birds seen on the plain.
At five feet in height with a wingspan of six,
To see one up close will give you some kicks.

Its plumage is gray with a crown of bright red,
With black bill and legs and white cheeks on its head.
Long, fluffy tertials hang over the tail
To fashion a bustle on both female and male.

With very long necks all stretched out in space
And legs straight behind, they fly with such grace.
In contrast, blue herons hold their necks in an S;
To tell them apart, you don't have to guess.

The birds mate for life and must like to dance;
They bow, jump and run and throw sticks and prance.
It's considered to be a large part of courting,
Yet all different ages go likewise cavorting.

Dancing is normal; it relieves their aggression
And also their tensions and any obsessions.
Adult birds will use it to lessen their cares
And strengthen the bonds between mating pairs.

They much prefer nesting in freshwater wetlands,
But utilize bogs to meadows and grasslands.
The dominant foliage is formed into nests,
Where two colts are fledged when parents are blessed.

The cranes will eat vertebrates, mice and small snakes
Plus seeds and invertebrates, whatever it takes.
They're also quite good at poking around
And finding what farmers have planted in ground.

The cranes are still common, abundant, and yet,
Habitat loss is the primary threat.
For migrating birds it's of greatest concern.
We need to protect it, lest they never return.

The Sand Hill Plum

Prunus angustifolia, the Sand Hill Plum,
Makes such a good jelly, you'll almost succumb.
It's sweet and it's tart when lavishly spread
On crescents and biscuits and just plain old bread.

It's the most common wild plum, mostly out west,
But it's certainly the one that I like the best.
It grows to a height of three to four feet
And sends out root suckers for thickets, so neat.

Elliptical leaves are folded lengthwise,
With tips curled down, two inches in size.
In April the thicket will blossom all white;
By July there'll be plums, red-orange and bright.

The plant is quite useful out where the wind blows,
It holds down the soil and helps make good wind rows.
As a wildlife shelter, it's quite hard to beat.
Oh, yes! Don't forget the good jelly to eat.

The Shagbark Hickory

Carya ovata is the Shagbark Hickory;
But it's also known as Shellbark.
It's certainly not taxonomic trickery,
But *C. laciniosa* is also Shellbark.

Long, loose plates of the bark
Flake off in a manner unique.
To see it you'd surely remark
That you'd know it with one little peek.

Leaves are pinnately compound
Twelve to fourteen inches long.
The four to six leaflets are crowned
With one standing dominant and strong.

Hickory nuts are edible fruits;
Round seeds with very thick cases.
Each one has four very clear flutes,
Which are transcribed onto the seed faces.

The nut-meat is sweet and delicious,
But the shell is as hard as a rock.
To crack them, you have to get vicious
And give them a very sharp knock.

The wood has a great many uses,
In handles for work and for play.
It can withstand the many abuses
Your hammer sees day after day.

The hickory has been used by mankind
Ever since we made our debut.
Its essence enjoyed as we dined
On smoked meat from the old barbecue.

The Skunk

Mephitis mephitis is the "polecat," the Skunk.
If you sneak up behind one, you'll get in a funk.
They're very attractive with black and white stripes,
But if you surprise one, you'll need perfumed wipes.

Their most prominent feature is their anal scent glands.
A great deal of respect is what they command.
Adjacent muscles allow them to spray
The scent from seven to ten feet away.

The skunk carries ammo for five or six uses
And it takes up to ten days to replenish these juices.
So they're quite reluctant to use this defense;
They rely on their colors to jog your good sense.

Most normal predators leave skunks alone
For fear of receiving a dose of cologne.
The great horned owl thinks that skunks are just swell,
Because owls, like most birds, have a poor sense of smell.

Two different thiols produce the strong smell.
They're so overpowering, that's how they repel.
You can detect the scent from a mile or more.
It's so very distinctive, it's hard to ignore.

The odor's not easy to eradicate.
With several home remedies, it's said to abate.
It's said that tomato juice works very well,
But even if you bathe in it, you're likely to smell.

The scent is not soluble, even with soap,
So resorting to chemistry is, by far, your best hope.
The thiols can be catalyzed into thiolates
With peroxide and bicarb, which works out just great.

Skunks are nocturnal, with good hearing and smell,
But they're very nearsighted, so don't see very well.
They'll walk in the road, ignoring the traffic
And have an encounter that's exceedingly graphic.

(Continued)

Skunks are omnivorous, but mostly eat meat
Insects and earthworms are their favorite treats.
They'll also eat vertebrates, like rodents and frogs,
But will get in your trash or the food for the dogs.

Whenever you see one, you'd best back away
Or you'll very likely express some dismay.
You can think that they're charming and cuddly and cute,
But they're quite deserving of their ill repute.

The Smallflower Verbena

Verbena bipinnatifidas is the Smallflower Verbena.
They're stunning additions to the wildflower arena.
It's an herbaceous perennial seen spring through the fall,
But if it's not freezing, it blooms anytime at all.

It's resistant to drought and does well in the sun.
It's a beautiful plant, just second to none.
It grows to a full eighteen inches in height.
The small five lobed flowers are pretty and bright.

The flower will be lavender, purple or pink,
Which butterflies flock to for a cool, nectar drink.
This gorgeous wildflower, which Nature presents,
Has one other value – in landscape accents.

The Snapping Turtle

Chelydra serpentina, the Snapping Turtle you see,
Is a formidable critter, I think you'll agree.
In ponds with mud bottoms is where they'll reside,
With plenty of foliage and places to hide.

Its shell is not smooth, but serrated and rough,
And with powerful jaws, it looks very tough.
They have long spiked tails and flexible necks
And can bite farther back than one would expect.

Since they can't fully draw back into their shell,
They'll use fierce displays, at which they excel.
For those who stray close, they'll meet snapping jaws
Or get lacerated by very sharp claws.

Snappers will rarely leave water to bask,
But continue to float while performing this task.
They will leave the water and move overland
To find home or nest, when conditions demand.

They need only mate just once in a while,
Which makes reproduction somewhat versatile.
The female stores sperm to use as she needs.
She'll lay eggs for years without needing to breed.

When eggs have developed, the female will roam
To find a good place for the eggs to call home.
She'll lay all her eggs in warm, sandy soil;
Then she'll depart – there's no motherhood toil.

In three to four months the turtles will hatch
And head for the water in a scrambling batch.
Until they grow larger, they'll suffer predation
From birds, fish and mammals, just all of creation.

The snapper's an omnivore; it'll eat what is dead
Or plants, fish or birds or small mammals, instead.
They'll devour small game fish and young ducks and geese,
But the damage is minor so these species increase.

They don't make good pets; they require much care.
Whenever they're handled, you should always beware.
To get close and personal, you'd better not linger
Or, quick as a heartbeat, they'll nip off your finger.

The Sunflower

Helianthus annuus, family Asteraceae,
Keeps its face into the sun for all the world to see.
It meets the rising sun each morn with bright and happy face
And as the sun arcs through the sky, the head will match its pace.

The head, an inflorescence, is a large composite flower.
It's really many small florets raised up to the nth power.
The many outer ray florets exhibit all the color;
Little inner disc florets make seeds to yield another.

The seed is like a clam shell, as small as you have seen,
That's in a class, botanically, of fruits called an achene.
Each achene contains one seed; the shell is somewhat sharp.
The pointed, dry and husky shell is called a pericarp.

The disc florets are all laid out in geometric fashion.
To understand just how it works, you need mathematic passion.
They spiral left and spiral right, a pattern quite precise.
To describe it without calculus could never be concise.

It doesn't take a genius to appreciate the flowers,
Especially *Helianthus* over which the rest it towers.
With a bit of education and an appetite to learn,
You'll come to know the wonders spread across the terra firm.

The Sycamore

Platanus occidentalis is the stately Sycamore.
It grows far and wide and adds to the décor.
With maple-like leaves and mottled complexion,
It's held in esteem and viewed with affection.

Its family is *Platanaceae*, an ancient tree clan,
That's survived through a one hundred million year span.
It has stood through the ages, fearless and bold
And can easily reach five hundred years old.

It grows very well in riparian locales,
By rivers and streams and other canals.
In just the right spot, it'll raise many cheers,
Reaching seventy feet in seventeen years.

It bows to anthracnose, a fungal disease,
Which defoliates limbs and makes unsightly trees.
When colonial men saw them, they naturally assumed
That these leafless clusters were "witch's brooms."

The fruits dangle down in a ball packed so tight,
But when the wind blows, the seeds take to flight.
Each seed is a tiny and winged achene
And each ball will contain a hundred-umpteen.

As the tree grows much larger, the brown bark will peel.
It flakes off in chunks, white under bark to reveal.
This feature's unique; you can tell at a distance,
Which tree's a sycamore with no need of assistance.

The Timber Rattlesnake

Crotalus horridus, a venomous snake,
Announces his presence with a vigorous shake.
At a meter in length, plus some added for fun,
You'll feel your heart pumping and feet start to run.

They hang out in forests and rugged terrain,
Where shade keeps it cool and damp from the rain.
You'll tramp through the timber from morning to night
And not see a rattler; a hiker's delight.

While less of a danger than some viper strains,
A Timber's quick kiss will cause damage and pains.
It varies the volume of venom injected,
But non-lethal bites can still get infected.

Just under each eye is a heat sensing pit.
It helps detect danger or prey to be hit.
It eats mostly mammals that wander too near,
But also eats frogs, snakes and birds that are dear.

When the snake sheds its skin, it's a strenuous battle,
But when all's said and done, it has a new rattle.
These horny segments, just loosely attached,
Provide a great warning, succinctly dispatched.

The species is threatened, so give them a break.
A dead Timber rattler makes ecologists quake.
In nature, each species has its role to play,
So enjoy the encounter, then back away.

The Turkey Vulture

Cathartes aura is the black turkey vulture.
Its stereotype is a part of our culture.
The cinema cowboy is quite sure in his head,
That those big black vultures are circling the dead.

They're circling, indeed, for something to eat,
But if they had found some, they'd be down on their feet.
They're riding the thermals and scanning the ground
For any dead carcass that's not yet been found.

The sun heats the prairie, the prairie the air,
Warm air floats skyward, the vultures to bear.
While soaring, they "drunkenly" tip left and right;
It's how they catch thermals to continue their flight.

They soar with their wings held tight in a V,
Technically, they're held dihedrally.
While dipping and turning in effortless flight,
Gray flight feathers turn silver as they catch the light.

The vulture possesses a great sense of smell
To find carrion on plains or in forests, as well.
He flies high to scan prairie to quite great extent,
But close to the ground to pick up a scent.

They circle the thermals to dizzying heights
So still you would think that they're runaway kites.
There are few other birds so graceful and spry
Who arrest your attention and capture your eye.

The Upland Sandpiper

Bartramia longicauda is the "shorebird of the prairie."
Compared to his cousins, this Sandpiper's contrary.
Most of his relatives live near the shore,
But the Upland Sandpiper's on the prairie, galore.

The bird's mostly brown, but barred dark and light
And its throat and its belly appear starkly white.
It has a long, slender neck, small head and large eyes
And his legs are bright yellow and long for his size.

They eat invertebrates and seeds, insects and grain,
Which they glean from the grass as they walk on the plain.
With stiff, fluttering wingbeats, their flight is unique.
When they land, they spread wings in a stretching technique.

They sit tight on their nest, with four eggs in the batch.
With the rest of the colony, they'll synchronize the hatch.
When the young birds have fledged, they start their migration
To South America and a pampa location.

The prairie in summer yields a concert of sounds
For those who get out and away from the towns.
The Upland Sandpipers will add to the show;
Their call's a wolf whistle, whr-r-reep, whreeeow

The Virginia Creeper

Parthenocissus quinquefolia, the Virginia Creeper,
Can climb any surface, from flatter to steeper.
Small pads on each tendril allows it to stick
To tree bark and siding, rock walls and brick.

The leaves are palmately compound, understand,
And spread like the digits of one of your hands.
With five leaflets, serrated, you'll readily see
The significant difference from poison ivy.

It flowers in the spring and fruits in the fall,
But it's mostly just birds that will eat them at all.
Oxalic acid is found in each berry.
It's toxic to mammals, so you'd better be wary.

It's planted for landscape, but is also a weed.
It's bright red in autumn, delightful, indeed.
It can cover your house so it's easy to cool,
But if you want to get rid of it, bring a sharp tool.

The Wavyleaf Thistle

Cirsium undulatum is the Wavyleaf Thistle,
Which grows over three feet in height.
Step on it barefoot and you surely will whistle
Or blue words your pain will incite.

It's a perennial weed found on dry, open land,
On roadsides and unsettled sites.
In overgrazed pastures, it'll make a fine stand;
It seems to grow just for spite.

The pinnatifid leaves are crowded and wooly;
The lobes are tipped with sharp spines.
In fact, the plant is spine-covered fully,
Like a pitchfork with hundreds of tines.

One urn-shaped head will terminate each stem
With flowers, from lavender to white.
As a noxious weed, this thistle's a gem,
In yards and pastures, a blight.

Birds eat the seeds and line nests with the fluff.
Thistledown is the term for the seeds.
Most animals find the thistle too tough
To satisfy their many needs.

When a thistle sprouts up in your manicured lawn,
To pull it is very unwise.
An herbicide dose will make it be gone,
Without bringing tears to your eyes.

The Western Painted Turtle

Chrysemys picta belli is the Western Painted Turtle in our streams,
Basking on logs, high and dry.
Lolling in the sun, while soaking up beams,
They're just watching the world amble by.

With a relatively flat and smooth carapace,
With the edges embellished with red,
This dark olive turtle has a yellow striped face,
But its limbs have red marks instead.

They much prefer water that is static to slow,
But rich in aquatic vegetation.
The pools should be based with thick mud below
To accommodate their hibernation.

To hibernate, they burrow into mud,
Which the turtles will find very pleasing.
A change then occurs to alter their blood
To survive at temps close to freezing.

Up to fifteen eggs the female will place
In soil that's sandy and loose.
The soil is packed down so as to erase
The nest to shield it from abuse.

If the eggs are kept at 82 degrees
Two-thirds of the young will be male.
When incubation occurs at 86 degrees,
Two-thirds will turn out to be female.

Eating insects and crayfish, carrion and plant-life,
The turtle's omnivorous, you'd say.
Whatever abounds, is part of its fief,
And comprises its varied buffet.

The turtle may steal the bait from your hook,
But they're more helpful than ever you'd guess.
They clean up the refuse from river or brook
To relieve environmental distress.

For the Western Painted Turtle to avoid a decline,
We must maintain high quality streams.
Healthy wetlands are integral to the design
Of our ecological schemes.

The White-Tailed Deer

Odocoileus virginianus, the ubiquitous white-tailed deer;
Was a food source for Indian and brave pioneer.
They range west from Atlantic to Pacific bright blue,
From far into Canada and south to Peru.

With four chambered stomach, like bison and sheep,
They swallow their food, but it doesn't go deep.
It's regurgitated; cud once again chewed;
Not at all appetizing, I think you'll conclude.

Brown-red in the summer, but with gray-brown fall coat,
They're white on the tummy, round the eyes, down the throat.
Their tail is a flag used to signal the fleet,
An appendage renowned, when forced to retreat.

Blessed with good eyesight, sharp hearing and smell,
If you get very close, you'll be doing quite well.
When they see you they'll bolt; they won't stop, look or glower,
But bound out of sight, forty miles to the hour.

The bucks wear the antlers, but does, not at all;
They're only for mating, during rut in the fall.
The does issue fawns; twin births are not rare.
The red fawns are mottled with spots of white hair.

Fawns stay with their mother for over a year.
They'll run in a group when taken with fear.
They'll rip through the timber, all hell bent for leather,
With white tail held high which will keep them together.

They never glance sideways 'fore bounding on road.
If your brakes aren't effective, your car will be towed.
So during the rut, well into December,
Stay watchful or have an affair to remember.

Glossary

Achene: a small dry indehiscent one-seeded fruit (as of a sunflower) developing from a simple ovary and usually having a thin pericarp attached to the seed at only one point

Aerie: the nest of a bird on a cliff or a mountaintop

Alternate: arranged first on one side and then on the other at different levels or points along an axial line <*alternate* leaves>

Anthracnose: any of numerous destructive plant diseases caused by imperfect fungi and characterized especially by necrotic lesions

Altricial: being hatched or born or having young that are hatched or born in a very immature and helpless condition so as to require care for some time <*altricial* birds>

Carapace: a bony or chitinous case or shield covering the back or part of the back of an animal (as a turtle or crab)

Carrion: dead and putrefying flesh; *also*: flesh unfit for food

Catkin: a spicate inflorescence (as of the willow, birch, or oak) bearing scaly bracts and unisexual usually apetalous flowers

Cephalothorax: the united head and thorax of an arachnid or higher crustacean

Chitin: a horny polysaccharide $(C_8H_{13}NO_5)_n$ that forms part of the hard outer integument especially of insects, arachnids, and crustaceans

Cloaca: the common chamber into which the intestinal and urogenital tracts discharge especially in monotreme mammals, birds, reptiles, amphibians

Coterie: an intimate and often exclusive group of persons (or animals) with a unifying common interest or purpose

Chrysalis: the enclosing case or covering of a pupa

Deciduous: falling off or shed seasonally or at a certain stage of development in the life cycle <*deciduous* leaves> <*deciduous* scales>

Dihedral: the angle between an aircraft (or bird) supporting surface (as a wing) and a horizontal transverse line

Dioecious: **1** : having male reproductive organs in one individual and female in another; **2** : having staminate and pistillate flowers borne on different individuals

Drupe: a one-seeded indehiscent fruit having a hard bony endocarp, a fleshy mesocarp, and a thin exocarp that is flexible (as in the cherry) or dry and almost leathery (as in the almond)

Fauna: animal life; *especially*: the animals characteristic of a region, period, or special environment

Flora: plant or bacterial life; *especially*: such life characteristic of a region, period, or special environment <fossil *flora*> <intestinal *flora*>

Floret: a small flower; *especially*: one of the small flowers forming the head of a composite plant

Funnelform: having the form of a funnel or cone <*funnelform* flowers>

Gestation: the carrying of young in the uterus

Hemipene: the bi-lobed male reproductive organs in most reptiles, kept invertedin the tail until needed.

Hypostome: any of several structures associated with the mouth; as **a:** the manubrium of a hydrozoan; **b:** a rodlike organ that arises at the base of the beak in various mites and ticks.

Inflorescence: **a:** the mode of development and arrangement of flowers on an axis; **b:** a floral axis with its appendages;

Infusion: a product obtained by steeping in liquid (as water) without boiling so as to extract the soluble constituents or principles <herbal *infusions*>

Insectivorous: feeding on insects

Instar: a stage in the life of an arthropod (as an insect) between two successive molts; *also* : an individual in a specified instar

Lamella: a thin flat scale, membrane, or layer:

Lanceolate: tapering to a point at the apex and sometimes at the base <*lanceolate* leaves>

Leaflet: one of the divisions of a compound leaf

Legume: **1** : any of a large family (Leguminosae syn. Fabaceae, the legume family) of dicotyledonous herbs, shrubs, and trees having fruits that are legumes (sense 2) or loments, bearing nodules on the roots that contain nitrogen-fixing bacteria, and including important food and forage plants (as peas, beans, or clovers)
2 : a dry dehiscent one-celled fruit developed from a simple superior ovary and usually dehiscing into two valves with the seeds attached to the ventral suture

Lek: an assembly area where animals (as the prairie chicken) carry on display and courtship behavior; *also* : an aggregation of animals assembled on a lek for courtship

Lepidoptera: insects that are any of a large order (Lepidoptera) of insects comprising the butterflies, moths, and skippers that as adults have four broad or lanceolate wings usually covered with minute overlapping and often brightly colored scales and that as larvae are caterpillars

Loam: a soil consisting of a friable mixture of varying proportions of clay, silt, and sand

Monogamous: the condition or practice of having a single mate during a period of time

Monotreme: any of an order (Monotremata) of egg-laying mammals comprising the platypuses and echidnas

Musk: a substance with a penetrating persistent odor obtained from a sac beneath the abdominal skin of the male musk deer and used as a perfume fixative; *also* : a similar substance from another animal or a synthetic substitute

Nocturnal: **1** : of, relating to, or occurring in the night <a *nocturnal* journey>

    2 : active at night <a *nocturnal* predator>

Nut: a dry indehiscent one-seeded fruit with a woody pericarp

Nymph: any of various immature insects; *especially* : a larva of an insect (as a grasshopper, true bug, or mayfly) with incomplete metamorphosis that differs from the imago especially in size and in its incompletely developed wings and genitalia

Omnivorous: feeding on both animal and vegetable substances

Opposite: arranged one above or alongside the other

Ovate: having an outline like a longitudinal section of an egg with the basal end broader <*ovate* leaves>

Ovoviviparous: producing eggs that develop within the maternal body (as of various fishes or reptiles) and hatch within or immediately after release from the parent

Palmately Compound: resembling a hand with the fingers spread: as having lobes radiating from a common point <a *palmate* leaf>

Pericarp: the ripened and variously modified walls of a plant ovary

Petiole: a slender stem that supports the blade of a foliage leaf

Pinnately Compound: resembling a feather especially in having similar parts arranged on opposite sides of an axis like the barbs on the rachis of a feather <a *pinnate* leaf>

Pinnatifid: cleft in a pinnate manner <a *pinnatifid* leaf>

Plastron: the ventral part of the shell of a tortoise or turtle consisting typically of nine symmetrically placed bones overlaid by horny plates

Polygyny: the state or practice of having more than one wife or female mate at a time

Precocial: capable of a high degree of independent activity from birth <ducklings are *precocial*>

Prehensile: adapted for seizing or grasping especially by wrapping around <*prehensile* tail>

Rhizome: a somewhat elongate usually horizontal subterranean plant stem that is often thickened by deposits of reserve food material, produces shoots above and roots below, and is distinguished from a true root in possessing buds, nodes, and usually scalelike leaves

Riparian: relating to or living or located on the bank of a natural watercourse (as a river) or sometimes of a lake or a tidewater <*riparian* trees>

Samara: a dry indehiscent usually one-seeded winged fruit (as of an ash or elm tree)

Scat: an animal fecal dropping

Scute: an external bony or horny plate or large scale

Serrate: a formation resembling the toothed edge of a saw

Serrated: to mark or make with serrations <a *serrated* knife>

Simple: not subdivided into branches or leaflets <a *simple* stem> <a *simple* leaf> (2) : consisting of a single carpel (3) : developing from a single ovary <a *simple* fruit>

Spirochete: any of an order (Spirochaetales) of slender spirally undulating bacteria including those causing syphilis and Lyme disease

Stabilimentum: a structure in a web, the function of which is uncertain. It may serve to stabilize the web, but also camouflages the spider. The silk reflects ultraviolet light, so may be attractive to insects. It may also be used to wrap prey, being of the same silk used for that purpose.

Stamen: a microsporophyll of a seed plant; *specifically* : the pollen-producing male organ of a flower that consists of an anther and a filament

Tendril: a leaf, stipule, or stem modified into a slender spirally coiling sensitive organ serving to attach a climbing plant to its support

Tertial: Of, relating to, or designating the third row of flight feathers on the basal section of a bird's wing. A tertial feather.

Thiol: any of various compounds having the general formula RSH which are analogous to alcohols but in which sulfur replaces the oxygen of the hydroxyl group and which have disagreeable odors

Thiolate: the deprotonated form RS^- (called a thiolate) is more chemically reactive than the protonated thiol form RSH.

Thorax: the middle of the three chief divisions of the body of an insect; *also* : the corresponding part of a crustacean or an arachnid

Thyrse: a staff surmounted by a pinecone or by a bunch of vine or ivy leaves with grapes or berries

Tillershoot: a shoot, especially one from the base of a plant or from the axils of its lower leaves

Tymbal: the vibrating membrane in the shrilling organ of a cicada

Tympana: a thin tense membrane covering an organ of hearing of an insect

Umbrel: a racemose inflorescence typical of the carrot family in which the pedicels arise from about the same point to form a flat or rounded flower cluster

Wattles: a fleshy pendulous process usually about the head or neck (as of a bird)

Appendix A

Beaver

I was a member of the Boy Scouts throughout most of my youth. When I transferred to the troop at the Methodist Church, I advanced faster than I had prior to my transfer. Jim Dancer was the scoutmaster and encouraged us to earn merit badges and other awards, one of which was a 50 Mile Canoeing award. Five or six of us decided to earn the canoeing award one late November weekend. We were to canoe the Neosho river from Burlington to Chanute.

We launched our canoes just below the dam at Burlington. The water was fairly shallow and swift at that point and we had to canoe through some narrows. As we rounded the gravel bar and entered swift water, we discovered a tree lying across the narrow waterway about 18" above the water. We barely averted disaster less than 50 yards from our point of departure. The rest of the trip, fortunately, was less harrowing.

For the most part, the Neosho river is deep and slow. To canoe the river requires paddling virtually the entire way. Being young, able bodied high school boys, we were certainly up to the task and soon became expert canoeists. Our primary problem was getting to gravel bars in time to make camp and prepare meals. Much of our travel would occur after dark since gravel bars are few and far between along that stretch of the river. Fortunately the sky was crystal clear and the moon was full although the air was a chilly.

Canoes are very quiet when slipping through the water so we'd often come upon beavers unawares. As we'd silently approach, they would become aware of our presence, slap their tails against the water's surface as a warning and dive below the surface. We were treated to this performance many times from sundown until we finally would make camp.

Appendix B

Black Rat Snake

My wife Sandy and I had just purchased our first house in Lawrence. We lived in an area that at that time was bounded on the west by farm land. As such, we were often treated to the presence of wildlife.

One evening as I came home from work, I discovered a beautiful black rat snake in the shrubs outside our front door. Having been a snake lover for many years, I couldn't resist picking it up. As I was admiring it and not being too conscientious about how I was handling it, the snake decided to register his disapproval at being accosted.

It was as if time had been altered and everything was moving in slow motion. The snake very slowly extended his head and clamped down on my left thumb. I saw it coming, but I just couldn't seem to move fast enough to avoid the bite. The bite itself didn't hurt, but I had a reaction to the saliva in the wound. I spent the entire night lying on the cool bathroom floor trying to stop the excessive sweating that resulted. It wasn't the first time that I had been bitten by a snake, but it was the only time I had an adverse reaction.

Appendix C

Copperhead

My eldest daughter, Kylee, followed in my footsteps by developing a love of science, especially biology. She has been a high school biology teacher since graduating from KU. During high school and early college, she was a councilor at a nature day camp for elementary children called the Outdoor Education Laboratory. The children were exposed to various plants and animals, learned natural history and gained an appreciation for nature.

One afternoon after the children had left for the day, Kylee and the other councilors were preparing to release a timber rattlesnake back into the wild. Since it is an endangered species, they were not allowed to keep it. They had the rattlesnake in a cage with a copperhead.

While removing the rattlesnake, the copperhead also got loose. Obviously, they couldn't let it remain free, so Kylee was tasked with retrieving it. As she was recapturing it, she pinned it against the floor with a snake hook. She didn't use the hook as designed because (she said) she didn't want to hurt the snake. As she was picking it up, the copperhead slipped out from under the hook and nipped her on the left index finger.

Against her wishes, she was taken to the nearest hospital where they administered antivenin. She immediately had an anaphylactic reaction to the antivenin and spent the night in ICU. Her arm swelled up from her hand to her face. She developed a necrotic area on her finger, like a huge blood blister, about the size of a fifty cent piece. She ended up spending a week in the hospital and about six months in physical therapy from that little nip.

Copperheads in this area are not as venomous as they are in other parts of the country. Had she been bitten on the leg, treatment probably wouldn't have been necessary since the muscle mass would have been sufficient to accommodate the swelling. With a bite on the hand, the resultant swelling could inhibit blood flow to the area. That lack of blood flow can cause the loss of fingers or even the entire hand.

Kylee still is as enthusiastic about biology as ever. She has participated in studies of snakes where they were caught, measured, tagged and released. She will still handle venomous snakes, but she is much more careful now, as she should have been earlier. She keeps an Epi-Pen® handy in case she's bitten again.

Appendix D

Fox Squirrel

We live in an area that has mature pin oaks and a few black walnut trees, so squirrels abound. Several years ago, I noticed that a squirrel had gnawed through the cedar facia board and had gained entrance to the eave on one end of the house. The City of Olathe has an ordinance requiring the live capture of wildlife, so extermination was not an option. We obtained the services of a company to capture and release the squirrels so we could repair any damage they'd done. After checking the situation, it was discovered that they'd also gained entrance to the attic above the garage and the area above our front porch.

Traps were set at both ends of the house and over the course of five or six days, nine squirrels were captured, one of whom was a pregnant female. The young man who provided this service owned property south of Olathe where the squirrels could be released.

Once the destructive critters were removed, it was time to repair the damage. The gutters and downspouts were removed and the facia boards were replaced with cement board so they couldn't gnaw through it again. Other damage to the house was repaired, the area painted and new gutters installed. The total bill for it was in excess of $5,000.

In very short order, those cute little squirrels frolicking in the yard became those !@#$% tree rats!

Appendix E

Garden Spider

One early summer morning, I was fishing at the VFW lake south of Chanute. The property actually contains two nice ponds, rather than a lake. I was fishing in the smaller of the two, but decided to trek around the shallow end of the pond to get to a different fishing spot. Since it was still early, just after daybreak, the relative humidity was near 100%. As a result, there was a heavy dew on everything.

The south end of the pond is where the basin drains into the pond, so it's a bit boggy. There were a lot of cattails and small bushes through which I needed to travel. I went around one of those bushes and almost walked into the web of a garden spider. She had spread her net across the path through the area. The memorable thing about the encounter was that each fiber of the web was covered with small droplets of water. The web looked like a beautiful diamond necklace strung between the cattails.

A couple of hours later, the web would be just another spider web, but at that particular moment, it was a sight to behold.

Appendix F

Muskrat

One early spring morning, I went fishing at Olathe Lake in a cove at the northeast part of the lake. I was fishing from the bank when I noticed something swimming toward me from the back of the cove. When it finally came close to me, I discovered it was a muskrat. When it caught sight of me, it panicked and dived below the surface as muskrats will do.

A moment or two later, I noticed that the muskrat had been a female carrying a youngster in her mouth, but when she fled, she dropped the baby. The young muskrat slowly drifted toward shore where I picked it up. I lined a minnow bucket with a towel and placed the babe in it to await the return of Mom.

About a half hour later, the mother returned searching for her baby. When she got close, I tossed the baby out to her, but she again panicked and fled. The baby had also disappeared from view and I knew that the mother had not carried it away. I was afraid the youngster had sunk and would drown. Just then, I noticed the baby walking along the bottom of the lake and emerging at my feet. I again deposited it in the minnow bucket.

As I continued to fish, the muskrat again returned looking for her baby. This time, I merely set the baby on a rock at the edge of the water and took a position behind some shrubs to watch. As the adult swam by, the baby fell off the rock and was floundering around in the water. This commotion caught the attention of mother and she swam over to collect her missing child.

This was probably the most memorable wildlife experience I've had. All told, I was involved with that muskrat for close to an hour. Any thoughts of catching fish were far from my mind. My only regret was that my two young daughters had not been with me.

Appendix G

Northern Bobwhite

My brother in law, Bob, and I were dove hunting in an area southwest of Chanute one fall afternoon. As I was walking along looking for doves, I stepped into a covey of quail. There must have been 15 to 20 birds in the covey, all right under my feet.

When one quail takes off, it's wings are flapping so quickly that they make a lot of noise. When a covey flies, the noise is magnified. If you're hunting quail, you're prepared for it, but since I was dove hunting, quail was the furthest thing from my mind. When that covey flushed, I was startled beyond belief. It took a few moments for my heart rate to return to normal so that I could once again concentrate on doves.

Appendix H

Northern Water Snake

I've had three encounters with the northern water snake that were memorable. The first occurred years ago when I was fishing with my uncle Bud in the upper reaches of Toronto Lake on the Vertegris river. We were in Bud's boat crappie fishing late at night. He was in the bow chair and I was in the stern. All of a sudden, a huge splash erupted near me just outside the boat. Bud told me to keep an eye on the back of the boat. He had hardly finished the sentence when the aforementioned reptile peeked up over the transom.

I picked up a paddle and encouraged the snake to keep his distance. The snake decided that there was nothing worth his time, so it went on it's way. As it swam to the other side of the river, I noted that it was a good 6' in length. Bud was never a strong swimmer, but he said that if that snake had gotten into the boat, he would have bailed out. A prime example of the irrational fear of snakes many people have.

The second encounter occurred when my sister and her family were visiting. We boys decided to go fishing after supper. The party included my brother in law, Bob, his two sons, his son in law and me. Bob and I had hunted and fished together for many years, so it was a good time for us to enjoy time together.

We drove out to a low water dam called Brown Wells, which is north of Chanute. The sun was well down, but the moon was bright enough to see fairly well. I parked myself on the riprap below the dam and the rest of them were scattered down stream.

We hadn't been there long when someone yelled SNAKE. My response was that since I was there first, I wasn't about to move. A while later, I realized that things were certainly quiet. Only Bob and I were still fishing. The boys were back in the car. It appeared that they weren't all that interested in fishing, after all.

The third encounter was while fishing at Hillsdale Lake south of Olathe. I was slowly moving my boat through a stand of trees fishing for bass when I noticed a northern water snake climbing a tree - straight up. It was such an interesting spectacle that I quit fishing just to watch.

The snake would wedge himself between projectons of bark on the tree and using his ribs and, presumably, intercostal muscles, would inch himself upward. As he progressed, he would find another projection to push against and keep moving. It was phenomenal.

Appendix I

Red-Winged Blackbird

Our memories are the result of many things and all of our senses contribute to them. Sound and smell can form particularly strong memories. Once again, I was fishing at the VFW lake south of Chanute. I can still hear the squeak of the gate as it swung open.

Red-winged blackbirds were always abundant around the ponds, particularly the south pond with all the cattails in the shallow end. There were two large cottonwood trees between the ponds. The memory is still strong of blackbirds sitting in the lower branches of the trees and singing their hearts out.

Regardless of your reasons for being outside, the experiences gained while being out in nature are always worth the time spent.

Author Biography

Steve Moon graduated from the University of Kansas in 1968 with a degree in Education with a science concentration. Upon graduation, he taught 7th Grade science in the Wichita, KS school district. It soon became apparent that his interest did not lie in the teaching field, so he returned to pursue the degree in pharmacy that had been his initial goal. He graduated with a bachelor's degree in pharmacy in 1972. In 1978, he completed the requirements for a Master's degree in hospital pharmacy. His entire career was spent in hospital pharmacy, almost entirely in management positions.

He currently resides in Olathe, KS with his wife, Sandy. Mr. Moon can be reached at moon.steve@yahoo.com.